CODING & LOGIC WORKBOOK!

101 CHALLENGING, FUN CODING ACTIVITIES AND LOGIC PUZZLES FOR KIDS

JULIA DREAM

 **ACTIVITY 1**

In empty boxes draw the figures
according to their coordinates.

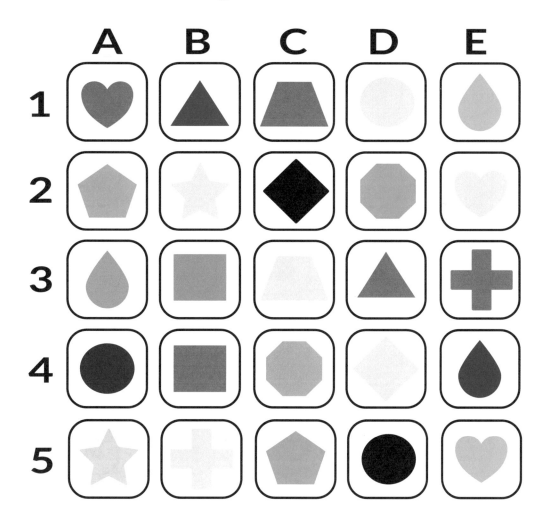

	A	B	C	D	E
1	heart	triangle	trapezoid	circle	drop
2	pentagon	star	diamond	octagon	heart
3	drop	square	trapezoid	triangle	cross
4	circle	square	octagon	diamond	drop
5	star	cross	pentagon	circle	heart

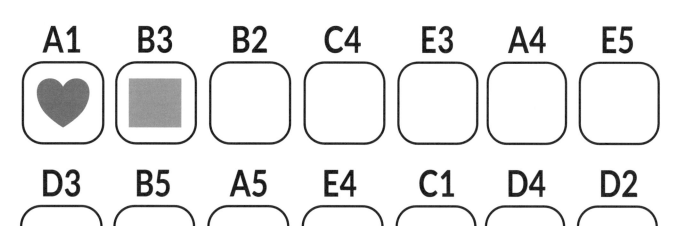

A1	B3	B2	C4	E3	A4	E5
heart	square					

D3	B5	A5	E4	C1	D4	D2

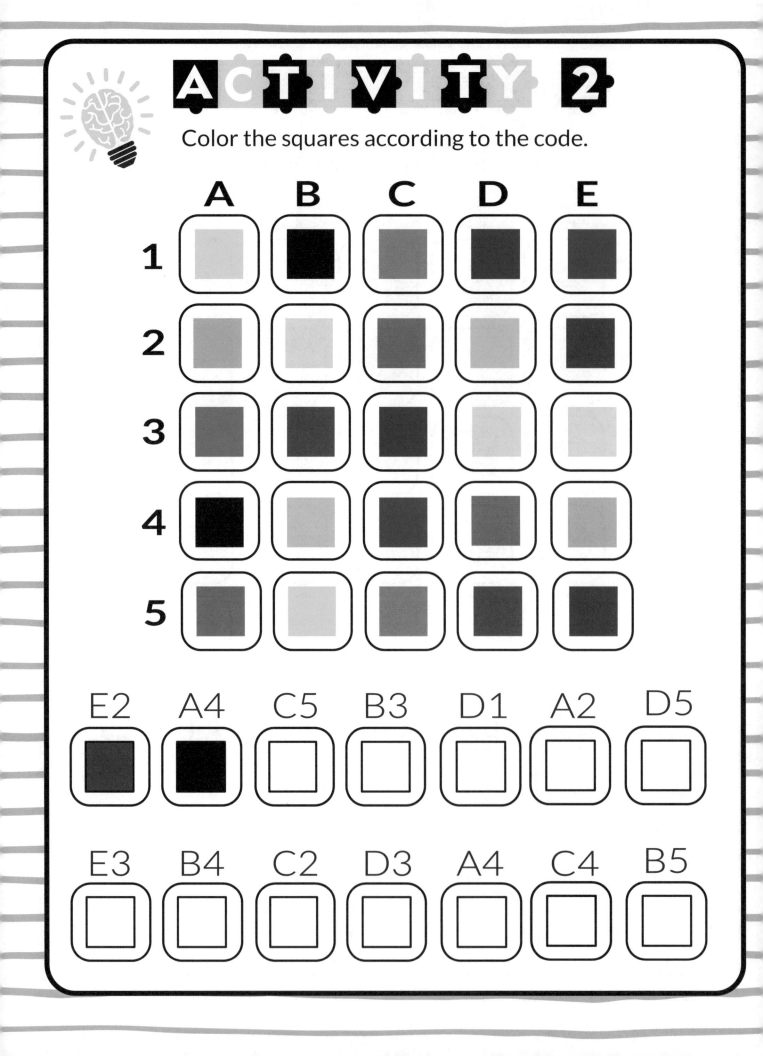

ACTIVITY 3

Complete repeating patterns.

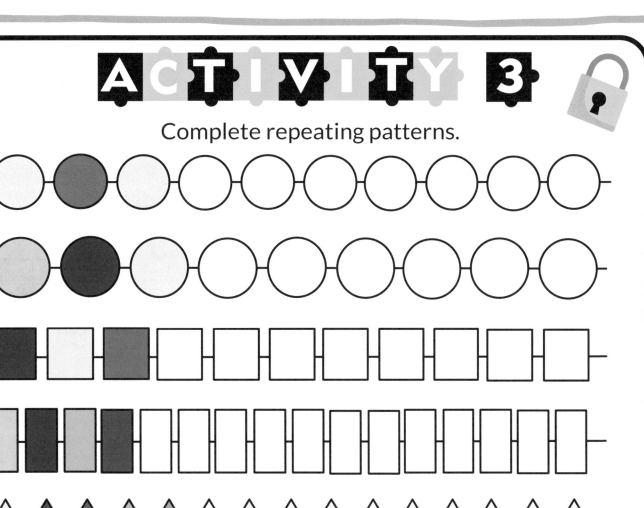

Draw the proper shapes in empty boxes and color them according to the code.

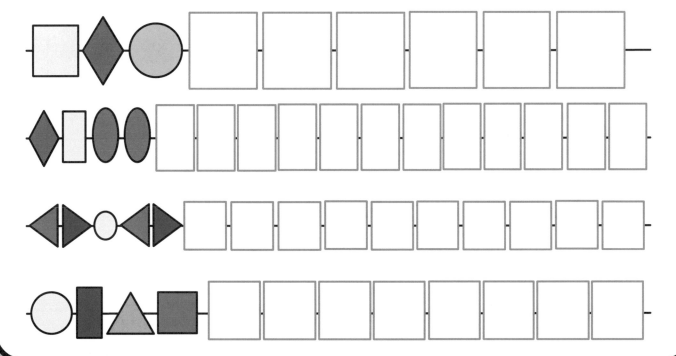

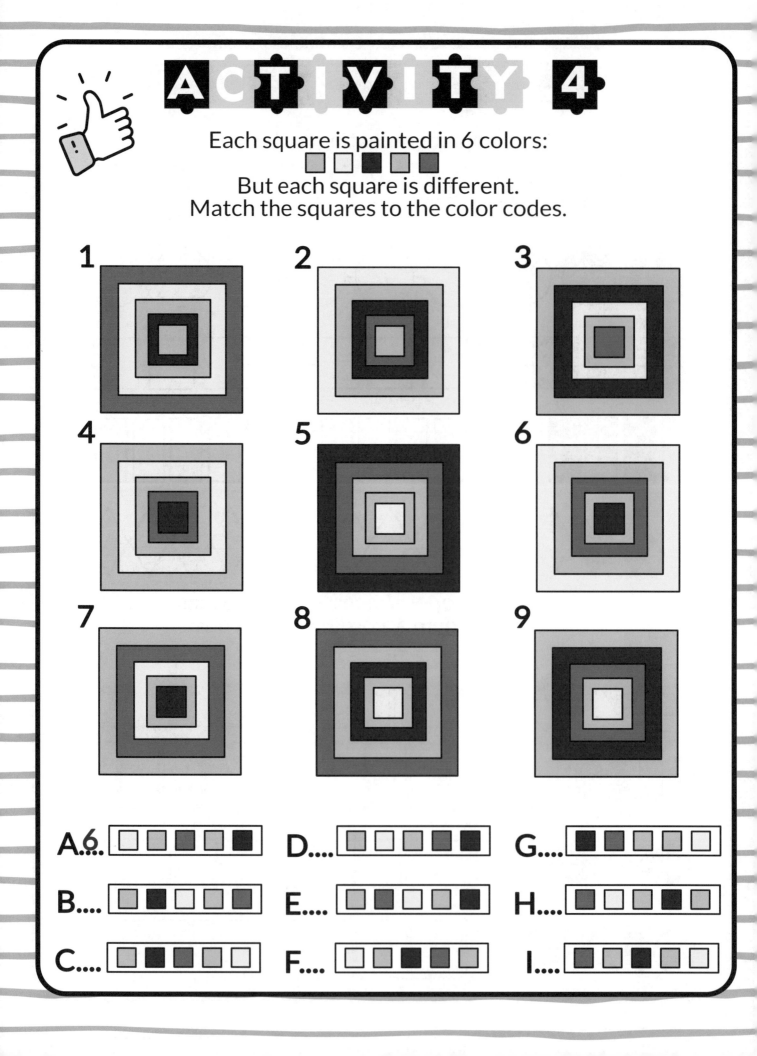

ACTIVITY 5

Color the circles in 6 colors:

Try to color each circle differently.
Create the color codes for each circle.

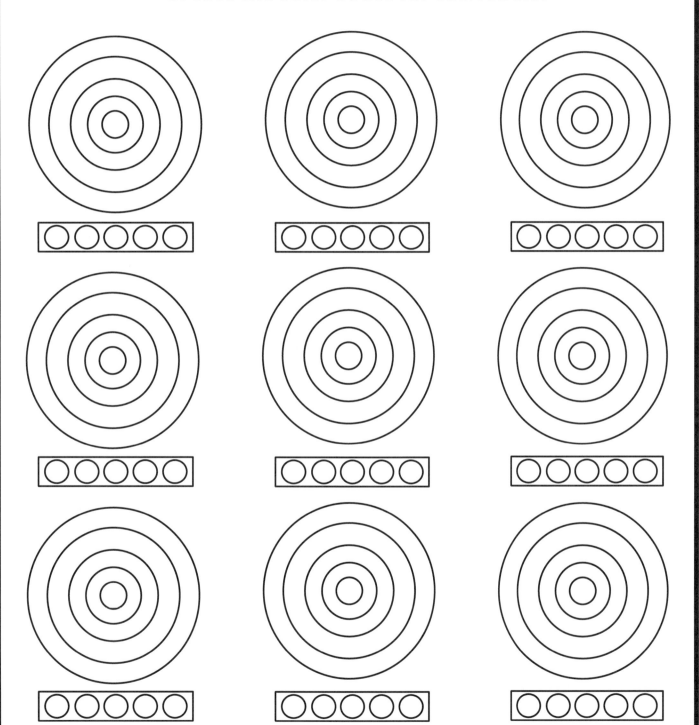

ACTIVITY 6

What are the small pictures coordinates?

F2   B7   ___   ___   ___   ___   ___

___   ___   ___   ___   ___   ___   ___

ACTIVITY 7

Where do these animals live?
Write the coordinates of their houses.

Animal	Coordinate
🐂	B5
🐷	
🦝	
🐨	
🦁	
🦥	
🐱	
🐘	
🐆	
🐶	

	A	B	C	D	E	F
1		🐶		🦝		🦊
2	🦁					
3		🐵		🦒		
4			🐱			🐼
5		🐂				
6				🦊		
7		🐆				🐨
8	🐻			🐘		
9					🦥	
10	🦝		🐷			

ACTIVITY 8

Finish the patterns.

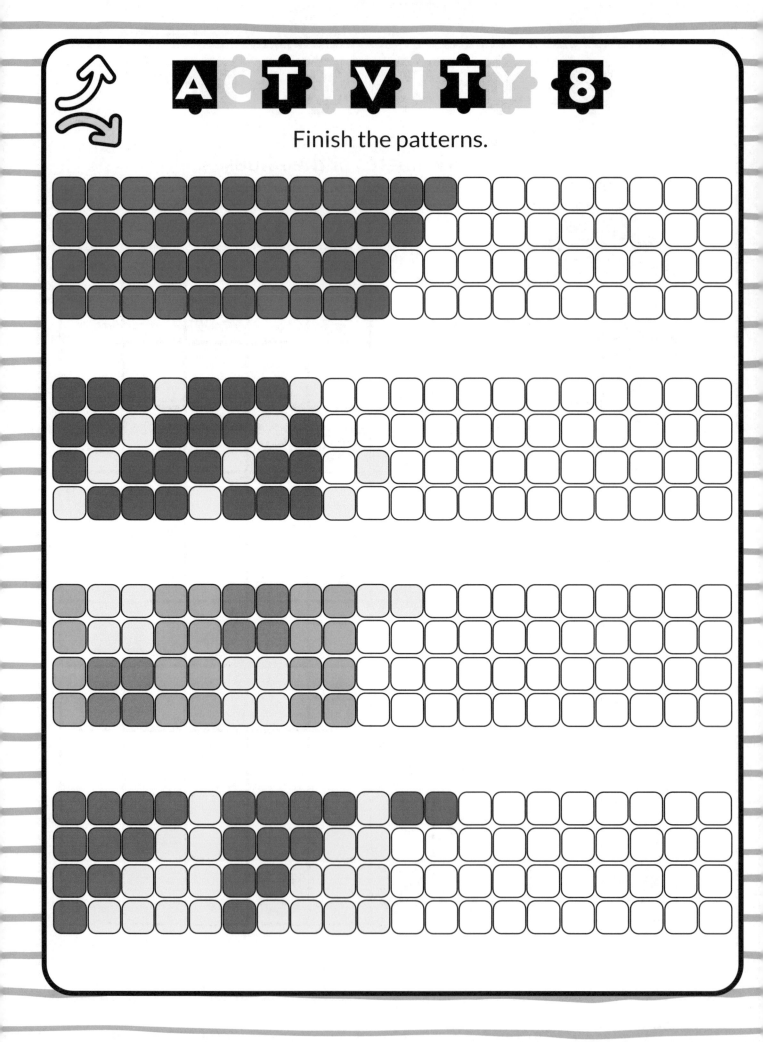

ACTIVITY 9

Copy the pictures.

Use the grid to complete the other side of the picture.

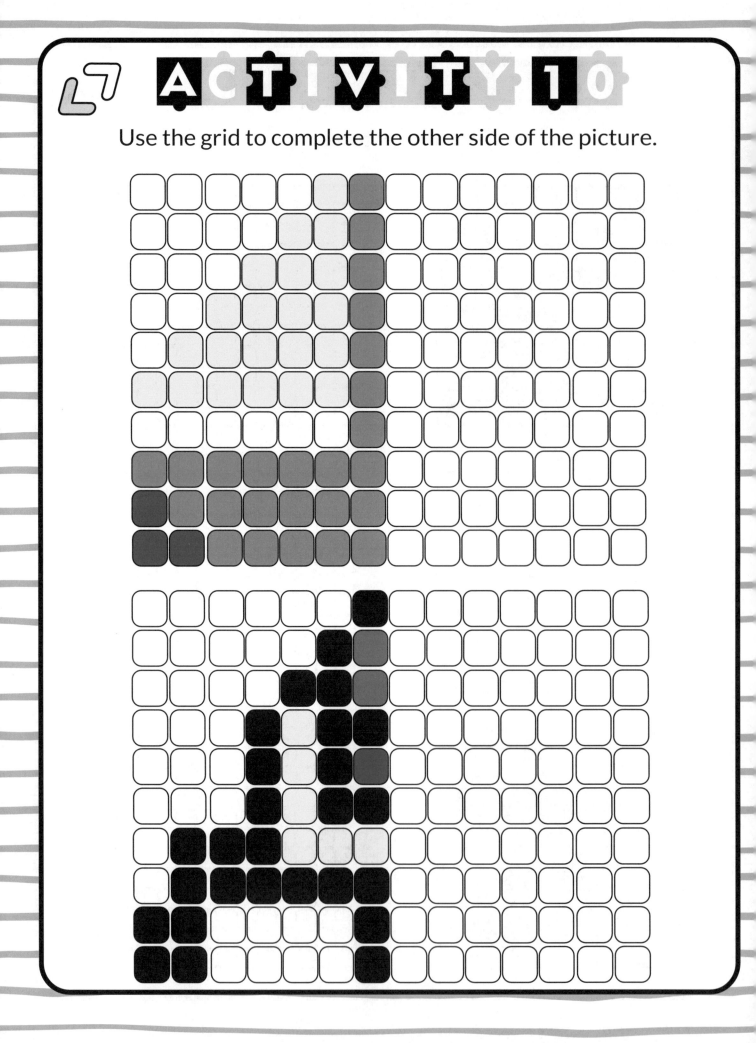

ACTIVITY 1

Use the code to color the grid and reveal the picture.

	A	B	C	D	E	F	G	H	I	J
1										
2										
3										
4										
5										
6										
7										
8										
9										
10										

○ A1, B1,C1, D1, E1, F1, G1, H1, I1, J1, A8, A9, A10, B9, B10, C10, D10,E10, F10, G10, H10, I9, I10, J8, J9, J10

● C5, D3, E7, F5, G3, H5

● A2, A3, A4, A5, A6, A7, B8, C8, C9, D9, E9, F9, G9, H8, H9, I8, J2, J3, J4, J5, J6, J7

● B2, B3, B4, B5, B6, B7, C7, D8, E8, F8, G8, H7, I2, I3, I4, I5, I6, I7

● C2, C3, C4, C6, D2, D4, D5, D6, D7, E2, E3, E4, E5, E6, F2, F3, F4, F6, F7, G2, G4, G5, G6, G7, H2, H3, H4, H6

ACTIVITY 12

Use the code to color the grid and reveal the picture.

	A	B	C	D	E	F	G	H	I	J
1										
2										
3										
4										
5										
6										
7										
8										
9										
10										

● E1, B2, C2, D2, E2, F2, G2, H2, E3

○ A1, A2, A3, A4, A6, A7, A8, A9, A10, B1, B3, B8, B9, B10, C1, C10, D1, F1, G1, G10, H1, H3, H8, H9, H10, I1, I2, I3, I4, I6, I7, I8, I9, I10, J1, J2, J3, J4, J5, J6, J7, J8, J9 10

● D3, F4, C5, H5, F6, D7, F8, D9

● A5, B4, B5, B6, B7, C3, C4, C6, C7, C8, C9, D4, D5, D6, D8, D10, E4, E5, E6, E7, E8, E9, E10, F3, F5, F7, F9, F10, G3, G4, G5, G6, G7, G8, G9, H4, H6, H7, I5

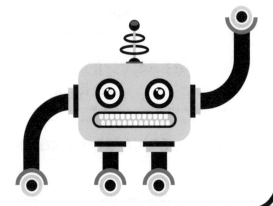

ACTIVITY 13

Use the code to color the grid and reveal the picture.

A B C D E F G H I J K L M N O P Q

1
2
3
4
5
6
7
8
9
10
11
12
13
14
15
16
17
18
19
20
21
22

A19, A20, A21, A22, B21, B22, C20, C21, C22, D22, E22, F22, G22, H22, I22, J22, K22, L22, M22, N22, O20, O21, O22, P21, P22, Q19, Q20, Q21, Q22

E18, E19, E20, F19, F20, F21, G10, G19, G20, G21, H9, H10, H11, H18, H19, H20, I9, I10, I11, J9, J10, J11, J18, J19, J20, K10, K19, K20, K21, L19, L20, L21, M18, M19, M20

B15, B16, B17, B18, B19, B20, C5, C6, C7, C8, C9, C14, C15, C16, C17, C18, C19, D4, D5, D6, D7, D8, D9, D10, D13, D14, D15, D16, D17, D18, D19, D20, D21, E3, E4, E10, E11, E12, E13, E14, E15, E16, E21, F3, F11, F12, F13, F14, F15, G2, G3, G7, G11, G12, G13, G14, H2, H3, H4, H12, H13, H21, I2, I3, I4, I5, I12, I13, I21, J2, J3, J4, J12, J13, J21, K2, K3, K7, K11, K12, K13, K14, L3, L11, L12, L13, L14, L15, M3, M4, M10, M11, M12, M13, M14, M15, M16, M21, N4, N5, N6, N7, N8, N9, N10, N13, N14, N15, N16, N17, N18, N19, N20, N21, O5, O6, O7, O8, O9, O14, O15, O16, O17, O18, O19,P15, P16, P17, P18, P19, P20

A1, A2, A3, A4, A5, A6, A7, A8, A9, A10, A11, A12, A13, A14, A15, A16, A17, A18, B1, B2, B3, B4, B5, B6, B7, B8, B9, B10, B11, B12, B13, B14, C1, C2, C3, C4, C10, C11, C12, C13, D1, D2, D3, D11, D12, E1, E2, F1, F2, G1, H1, I1, J1, K1, L1, L2, M1, M2, N1, N2, N3, N11, N12, O1, O2, O3, O4, O10, O11, O12, O13, P1, P2, P3, P4, P5, P6, P7, P8, P9, P10, P11, P12, P13, P14, Q1, Q2, Q3, Q4, Q5, Q6, Q7, Q8, Q9, Q10, Q11, Q12, Q13, Q14, Q15, Q16, Q17, Q18

ACTIVITY 14

Use the code to color the grid and reveal the picture.

A B C D E F G H I J K L M N O P Q

1 2 3 4 5 6 7 8 9 10 11 12 13 14 15 16 17 18 19 20 21 22

A1, A2, A3, A4, A5, A6, A7, A8, A9, A10, A11, B9, B10, C1, C10, D1, E1, E2, F1, F2, G1, G2, H1, H2, I1, I2, J1, J2, K1, K2, L1, L2, M1, M2, N1, O1, O10, P9, P10, Q1, Q2, Q3, Q4, Q5, Q6, Q7, Q8, Q9, Q10, Q11

A17, A18, A19, B18, B19, C19, O19, P18, P19, Q17 Q18, Q19

H8, H9, H21, I8, I9, I10, J8, J9, J21, D21, E21, F21, G21, K21, L21, M21, N21

A20, A21, A22, B20, B21, B22, C20, C21, C22, D20, D22, E22, F22, G22, H22, I21, I22, J22, K22, L22, M22, N20, N22, O20, O21, O22, P20, P21, P22, Q20, Q21, Q22

D5, D6, D7, E5, E7, F5, F6, F7, L5, L6, L7, M5, M7, N5, N6, N7

B2, B3, B4, B5, B6, B7, B8, B13, B14, B15, B16, C2, C3, C9, C12, C13, C14, C15, C16, C17, D2, D3, D9, D10, D11, D12, D13, D17, D18, D19, E3, E9, E10, E11, E12, E18, E19, E20, F3, F9, F10, F11, F19, F20, G3, G9, G10, G11, G19, G20, H3, H4, H5, H6, H7, H10, H11, H19, H20, I3, I4, I5, I6, I7, I11, I19, I20, J3, J4, J5, J6, J7, J10, J11, J19, J20, K3, K9, K10, K11, K19, K20, L3, L9, L10, L11, L19, L20, M3, M9, M10, M11, M12, M18, M19, M20, N2, N3, N9, N10, N11, N12, N13, N17, N18, N19, O2, O3, O9, O12, O13, O14, O15, O16, O17, P2, P3, P4, P5, P6, P7, P8, P13, P14, P15,P16

A12, A13, A14, A15, A16, B1, B11, B12, B17, C11, C18, D15, F13, F17, G15, I13, I17, K15, L13, L17, N15, O11, O18, P1, P11, P12, P17, Q12, Q13, Q14, Q15, Q16

C4, C5, C6, C7,C8, D4, D8, D14, D16, E4, E8, E13, E14, E15, E16, E17, F4, F8, F12, F14, F15, F16, F18, G4, G5, G6, G7, G8, G12, G13, G14, G16, G17, G18, H12, H13, H14, H15, H16, H17, H18, I12, I14, I15, I16, I18, J12, J13, J14, J15, J16, J17, J18, K4, K5, K6, K7, K8, K12, K13, K14, K16, K17, K18, L4, L8, L12, L14, L15, L16, L18, M4, M8, M13, M14, M15, M16, M17, N4, N8, N14, N16, O4, O5, O6, O7, O8

ACTIVITY 15

Robot Olivier and Robot Lucas love dinosaurs toys.
Unfortunately, their dinosaurs toys have been mixed.
Help Robot Olivier to pick up all his toys by following the code
in the top table. Then, count Olivier's dinosaurs.
The reamining dinosaurs belong to Lucas. Count them too.

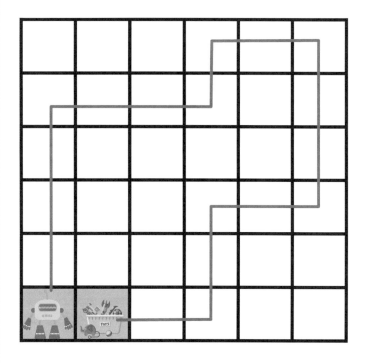

HOW MANY dinosaurs
does Robot Olivier have?

_____

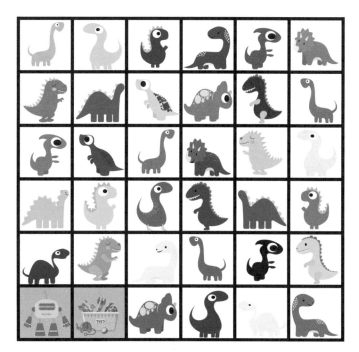

HOW MANY dinosaurs
does Robot Lucas have?

_____

ACTIVITY 16

Help Robot Olivier put his dinosaurs on the right shelves.
Write the first letters of dinosaurs' names
on the proper shelves by following the code.

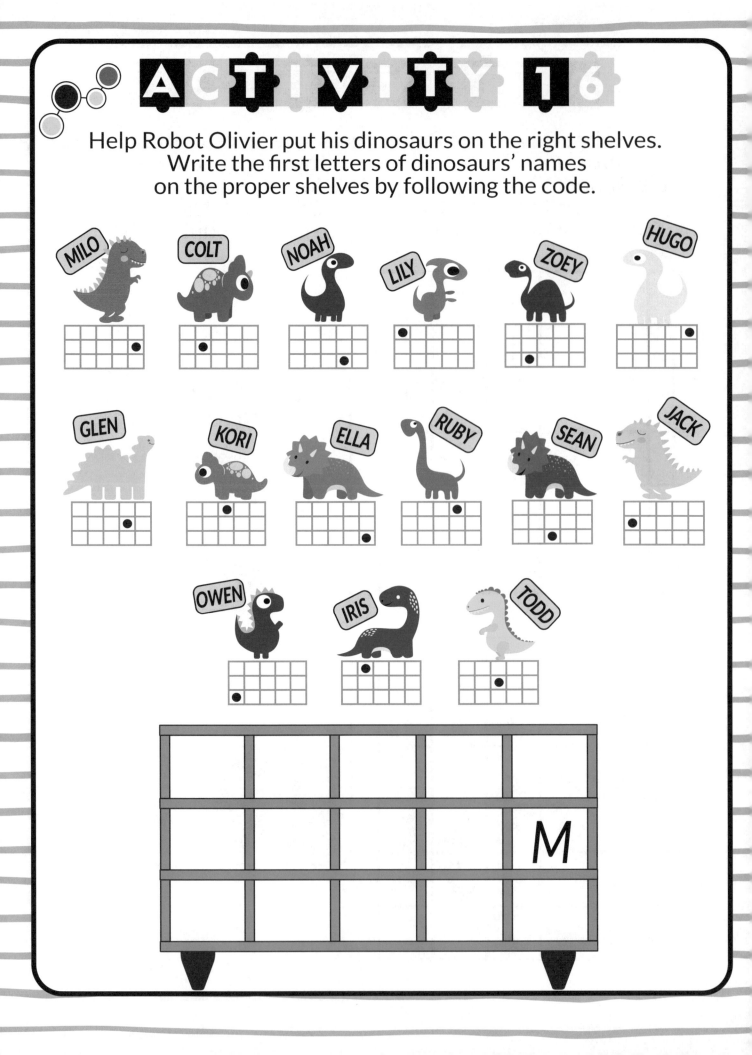

ACTIVITY 17

Robot LEO wants to get to his friend Alex. Draw the way according to the coordinates code below.

H8 , G8, F8, E8, D8, C8, C7, C6, D6,
E6, E5, E4, D4, C4, B4, B3, C3, D3,
E3, F3, F2, F1, E1, D1, C1, B1, A1

	A	B	C	D	E	F	G	H
1	ALEX							
2								
3								
4								
5								
6								
7								
8								LEO

ACTIVITY 18

Robot REX wants to get to his house.
Write the coordinates code for him.

	A	B	C	D	E	F	G	H
1								
2								
3								
4								
5								
6								
7								
8								

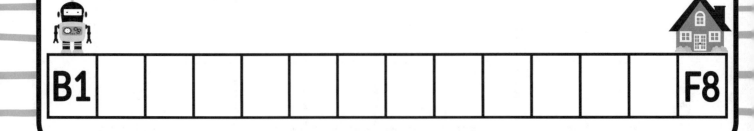

B1 | | | | | | | | | | | | | F8

ACTIVITY 19

Which arrow code is correct.
Put a ✓ in a correct square (grey, yellow or green).

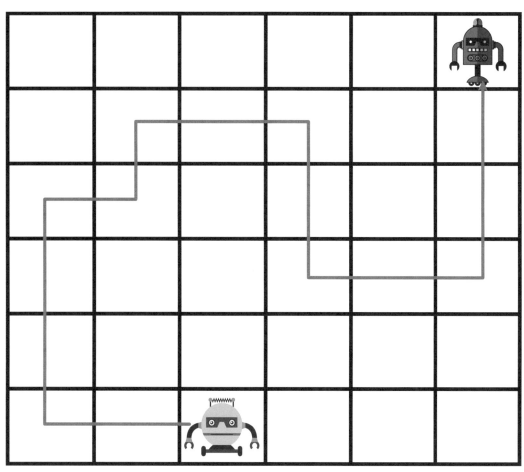

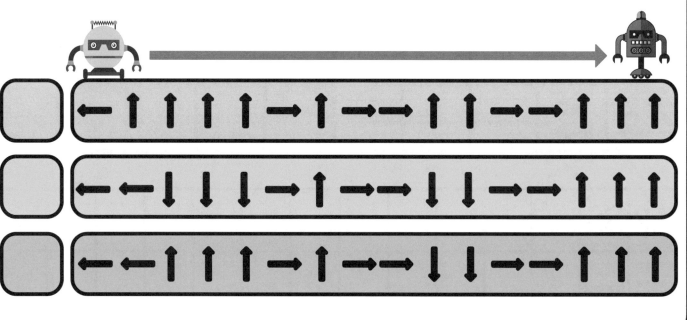

ACTIVITY 20

The robot CAT wants to catch the robot MOUSE.
Write the coordinate and arrow code for the robot CAT
according to the red line on the grid.

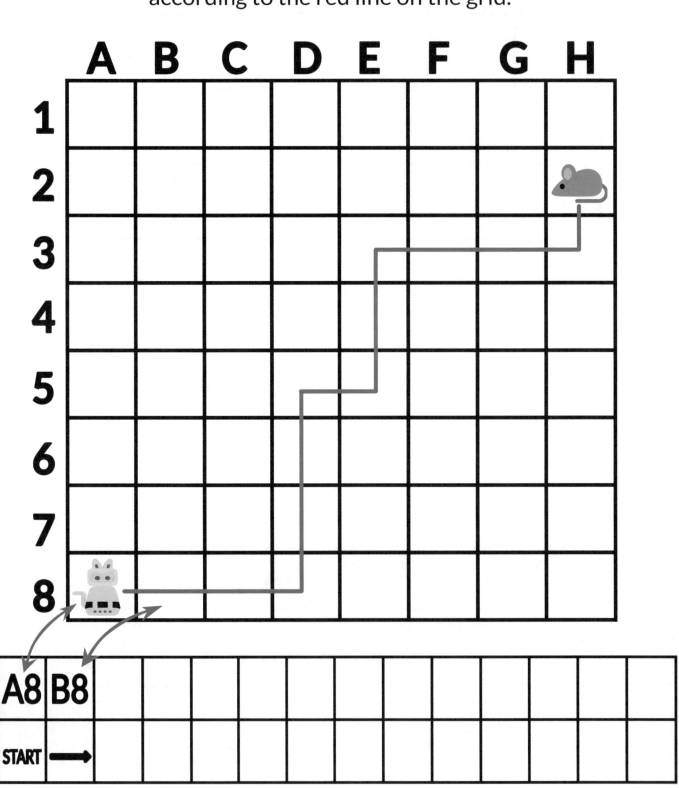

| A8 | B8 | | | | | | | | | | | | | |
| START → | | | | | | | | | | | | | | |

ACTIVITY 2

Whose toys are these? Decode the arrow codes to find out.

LIAM ↑↑↑↑→→↑↑→→→→↑←↑↑←

MIA ↑↑↑↑←←↑↑↑←←↑↑←

SOPHIA ↑↑↑↑→↑↑↑←←←↑↑→→

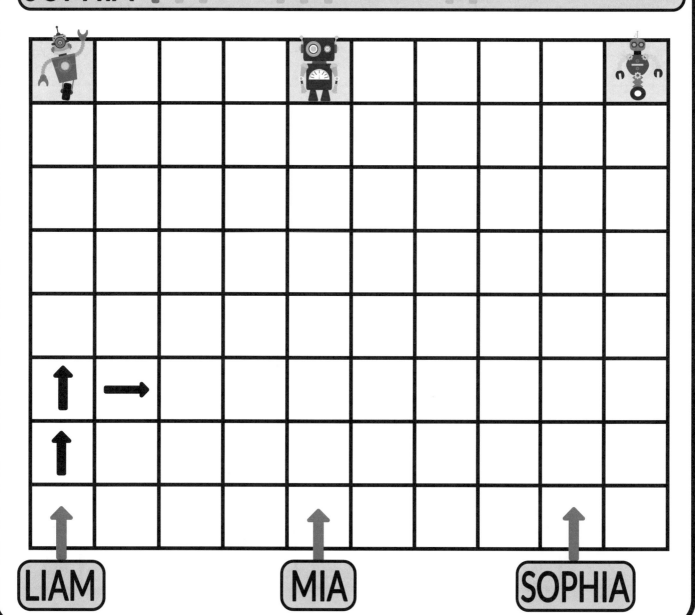

LIAM   MIA   SOPHIA

Whose toys are these? Decode the arrow codes to find out.

LUCAS	4→ 2↓ 3→ 2↓ 3→

HENRY	3→ 1↓ 3→ 2↑ 2→ 1↑ 2→

EMMA	2→ 1↓ 5→ 2↑ 3→

AVA	4→ 1↓ 4→ 2↑ 2→

ACTIVITY 23

Robots want to get to the Robot Party.
Write them codes around obstacles using numbers and arrows:

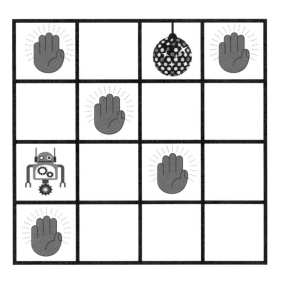

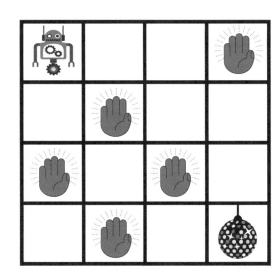

1→ 1↓

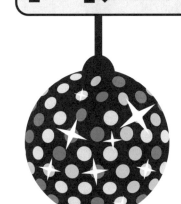

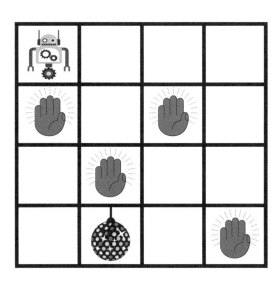

ACTIVITY 24

Robot MAX wants to pick all mushrooms in the forest.
Write him a code around obstacles using numbers and arrows:

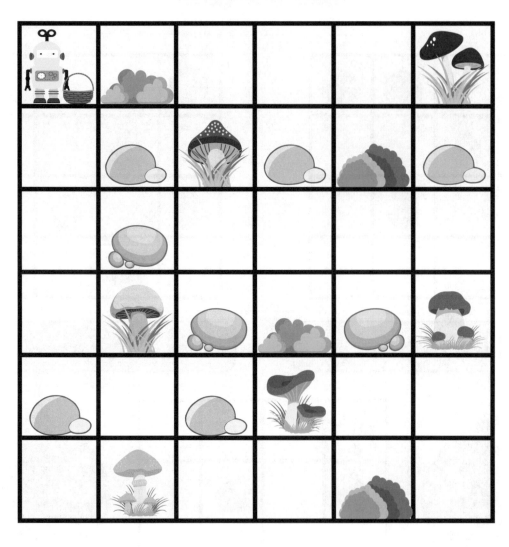

Decode the mystery sentence
according to the shape and number code in the grid.

	■	▲	●	💧	◆
1	J	E	Q	X	P
2	I	T	B	O	C
3	A	D	R	S	Y
4	H	W	F	Z	U
5	L	N	M	G	K

3◆ 2💧 4◆   3■ 3● 1▲

5💧 2■ 4● 2▲ 1▲ 3▲   3■ 5▲ 3▲

1▲ 1💧 2▲ 3● 3■ 2💧 3● 3▲ 2■ 5▲ 3■ 3● 3◆

ACTIVITY 26

Decode the mystery sentence
according to the shape and number code in the grid.

	■	▲	●	💧	◆
1	W	M	Q	P	E
2	A	T	U	O	D
3	H	J	G	K	Y
4	I	V	F	B	C
5	L	N	R	S	D

3◆ 2💧 2●   4◆ 2■ 5▲

- -

5◆ 2💧   5● 1◆ 2■ 5■ 5■ 3◆

- -

3■ 2■ 5● 2◆   2▲ 3■ 4■ 5▲ 3● 5💧

- -

Use the code to reveal the secret message for you.

YOU ARE A .....

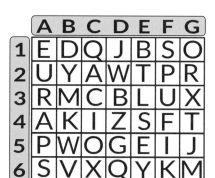

	A	B	C	D	E	F	G
1	E	D	Q	J	B	S	O
2	U	Y	A	W	T	P	R
3	R	M	C	B	L	U	X
4	A	K	I	Z	S	F	T
5	P	W	O	G	E	I	J
6	S	V	X	Q	Y	K	M
7	C	N	H	Z	F	L	A

	A	B	C	D	E	F	G
1	W	B	S	F	J	D	K
2	A	N	P	R	E	H	M
3	F	L	T	Z	X	G	E
4	P	A	Y	N	W	I	S
5	H	U	Q	O	Z	D	L
6	M	S	J	M	X	U	Q
7	G	O	K	C	I	A	W

	A	B	C	D	E	F	G
1	E	C	Y	B	J	D	F
2	A	F	Z	V	N	S	U
3	W	M	T	K	X	L	P
4	O	S	B	C	G	I	A
5	H	G	Z	D	F	O	K
6	B	S	X	A	Y	H	N
7	R	E	M	U	G	W	J

	A	B	C	D	E	F	G
1	B	S	X	A	Y	H	N
2	R	E	M	U	G	D	J
3	V	Y	K	C	I	A	W
4	C	I	Z	X	T	P	R
5	X	O	S	K	L	U	X
6	D	Q	J	B	S	D	K
7	Y	A	W	T	P	H	M

C3	F7	A1	B6	E5	G2
C					

B4	G7	E2	C1	D5	A6	G3

B1	A4	G6	G1	F4	D5	B7	E2	C3

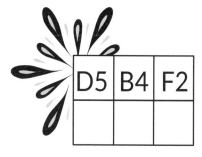

D5	B4	F2

ACTIVITY 28

Write the coordinates for each toy.

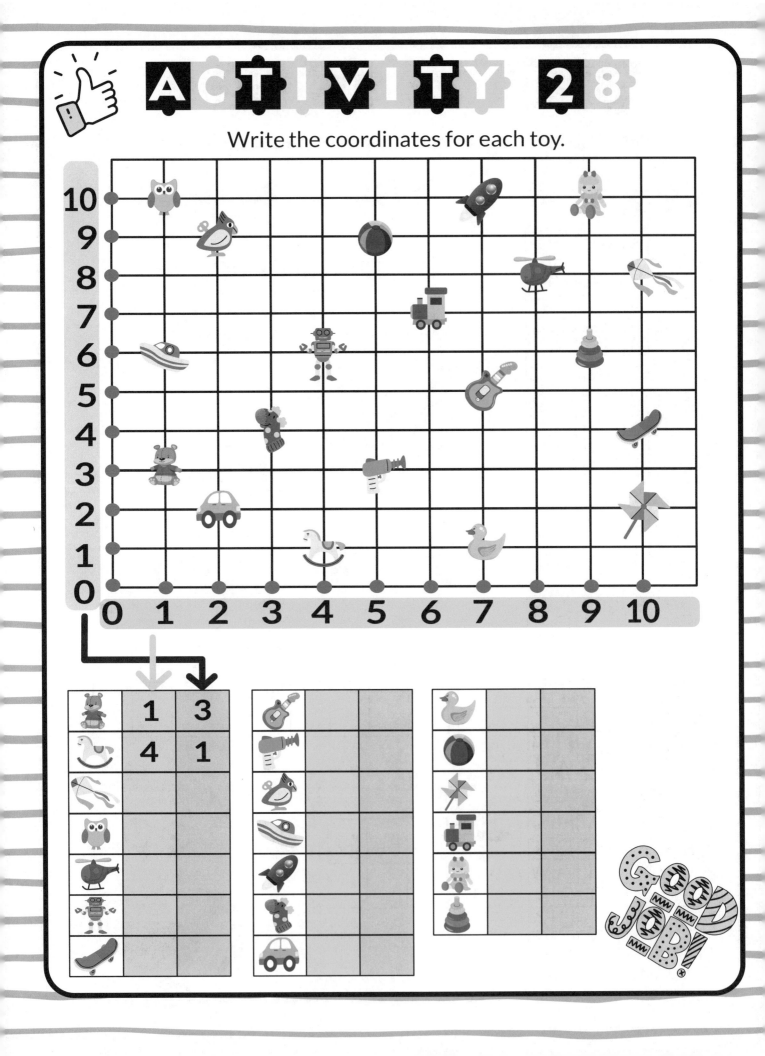

ACTIVITY 29

Write the coordinates for each fruit and vegetable.

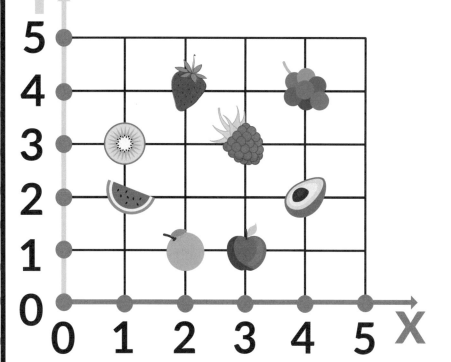

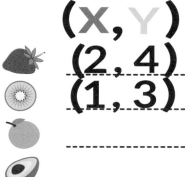

(X, Y)
(2, 4)
(1, 3)

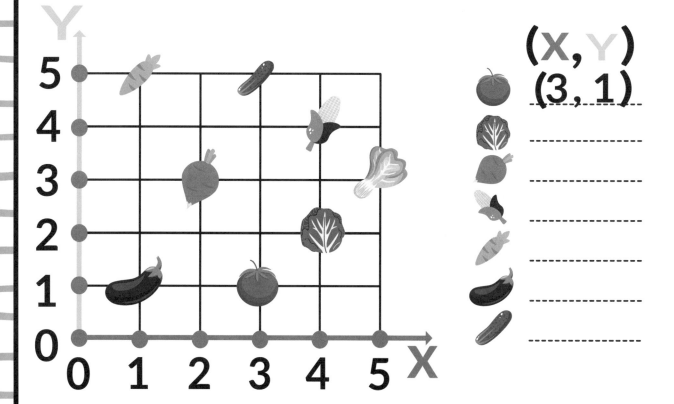

(X, Y)
(3, 1)

ACTIVITY 30

Plot the colorful circles on a coordinate grid.

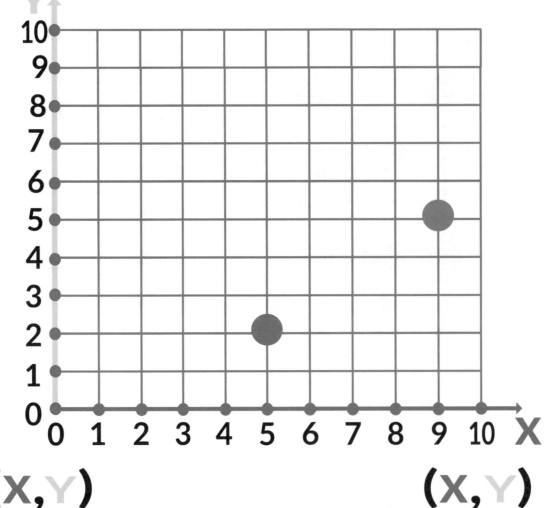

 (X, Y)

- (5,2) ....
- (9,5) ....
- (1, 10) ....
- (2,4) ....
- (5,6) ....
- (1,7) ....

(X, Y)

- (9,1) ....
- (7,8) ....
- (1,2) ....
- (9,9) ....
- (6,4) ....
- (4,8) ....

Plot the dots on the coordinate graph, join the dots to make shapes. Then, name the shapes.

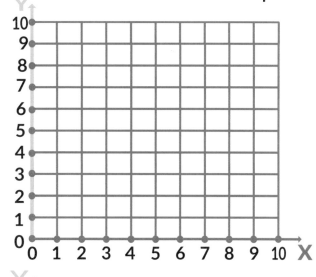

● (2,4)

● (7,9)

● (9,3)

SHAPE: ....

Is it a....

RECTANGLE

SQUARE

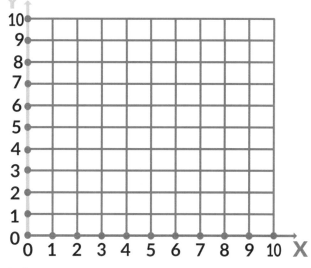

● (2,3)

● (2,8)

● (9,3)

● (9,8)

SHAPE: ....

TRAPEZOID

TRIANGLE

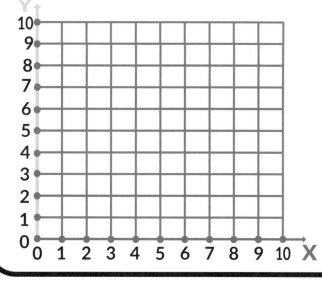

● (1,2)

● (3,6)

● (8,6)

● (10,2)

SHAPE: ....

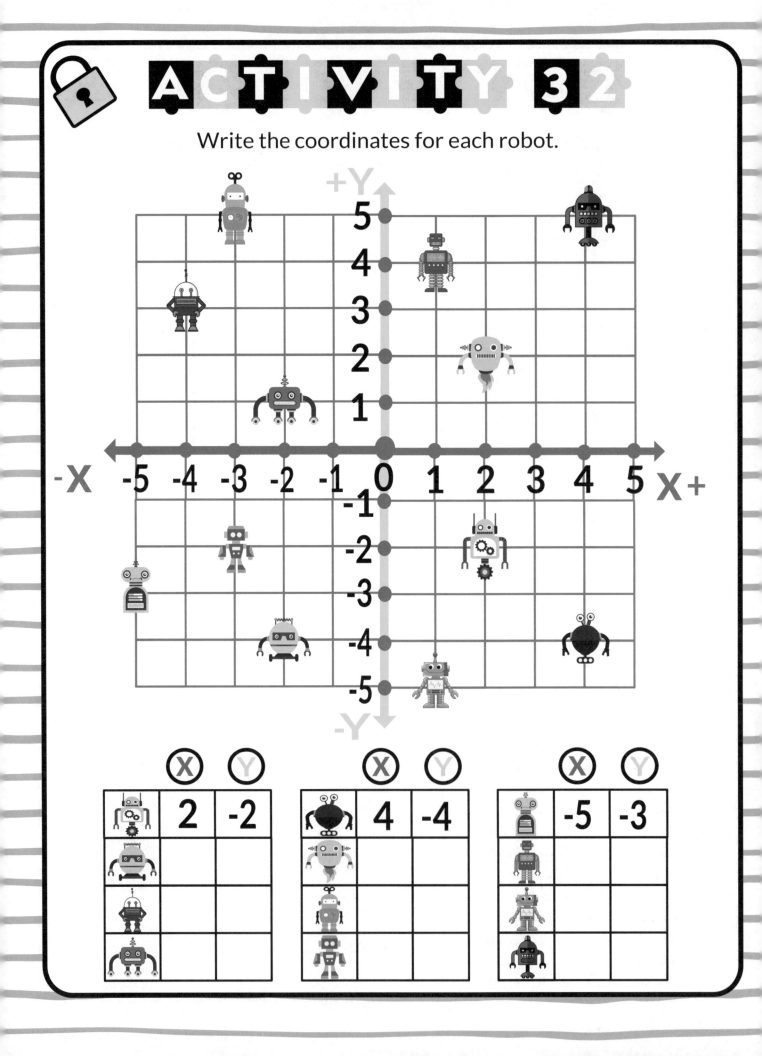

ACTIVITY 32

Write the coordinates for each robot.

Plot the following points on a coordinate grid, join the points from A to J to discover the mystery shape.

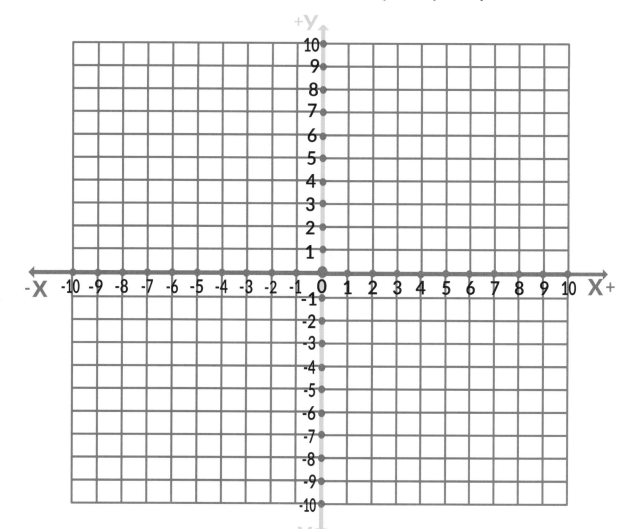

	X	Y		X	Y
A	(0,9)		F	(0,-5)
B	(2,2)		G	(-6,-9)
C	(9,2)		H	(-4,-2)
D	(4,-2)		I	(-9,2)
E	(6,-9)		J	(-2,2)

What is the mystery shape?

ACTIVITY 34

Plot the following points on a coordinate grid, join the points from A to V to discover the mystery shape.

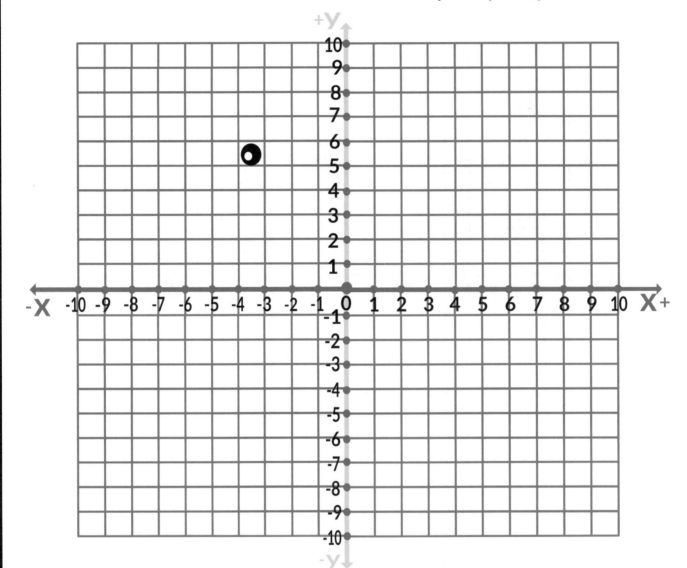

	X Y		X Y		X Y		X Y		X Y
(A)	(-1,5)	(F)	(2,-2)	(K)	(-4,1)	(P)	(-9,4)	(U)	(-4,7)
(B)	(3,5)	(G)	(2,1)	(L)	(-5,3)	(Q)	(-8,4)	(V)	(-2,7)
(C)	(5,3)	(H)	(-2,1)	(M)	(-7,2)	(R)	(-7,3)		
(D)	(4,3)	(I)	(-2,-2)	(N)	(-8,2)	(S)	(-6,4)		
(E)	(4,-2)	(J)	(-4,-2)	(O)	(-9,3)	(T)	(-5,6)		

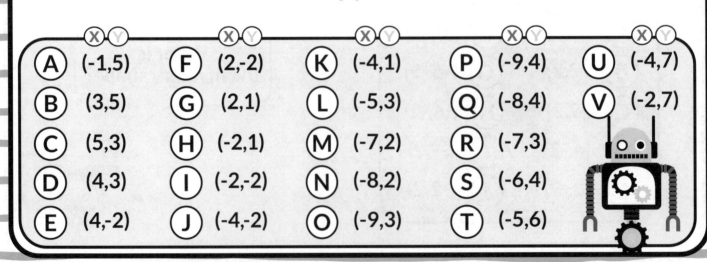

ACTIVITY 35

Decomposition. How many shapes can you see?

CIRCLES _____

SQUARES _____

TRIANGLES _____

RECTANGLES _____

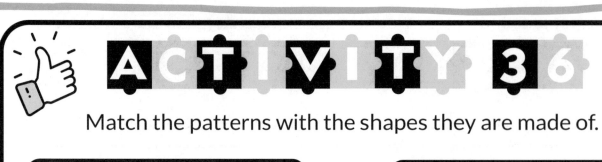

Match the patterns with the shapes they are made of.

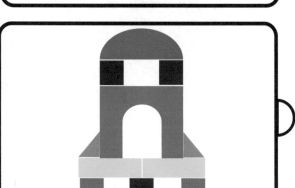

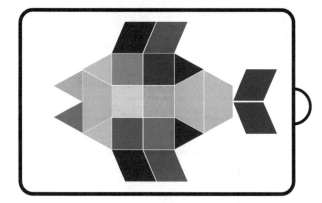
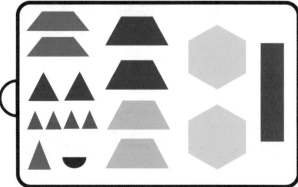

ACTIVITY 37

Count. How many shapes can you see?

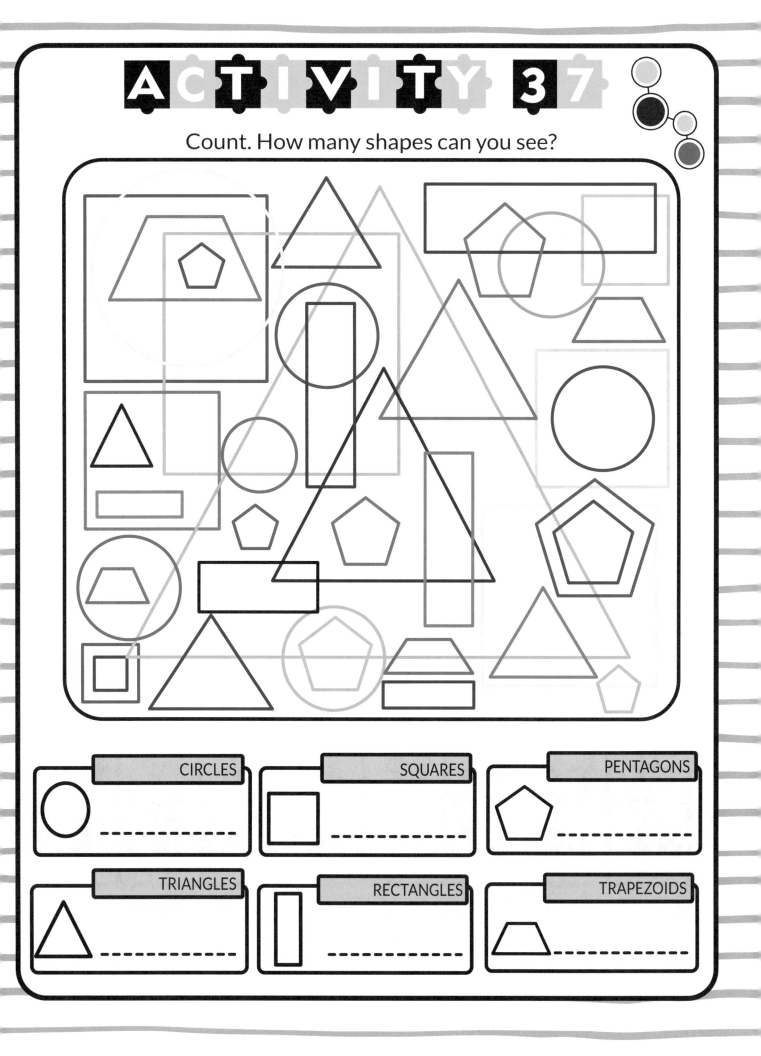

CIRCLES	SQUARES	PENTAGONS
_ _ _ _ _ _ _ _ _ _	_ _ _ _ _ _ _ _ _ _	_ _ _ _ _ _ _ _ _ _

TRIANGLES	RECTANGLES	TRAPEZOIDS
_ _ _ _ _ _ _ _ _ _	_ _ _ _ _ _ _ _ _ _	_ _ _ _ _ _ _ _ _ _

ACTIVITY 38

Gather all ROBO DOGS without taking the pen off the paper.

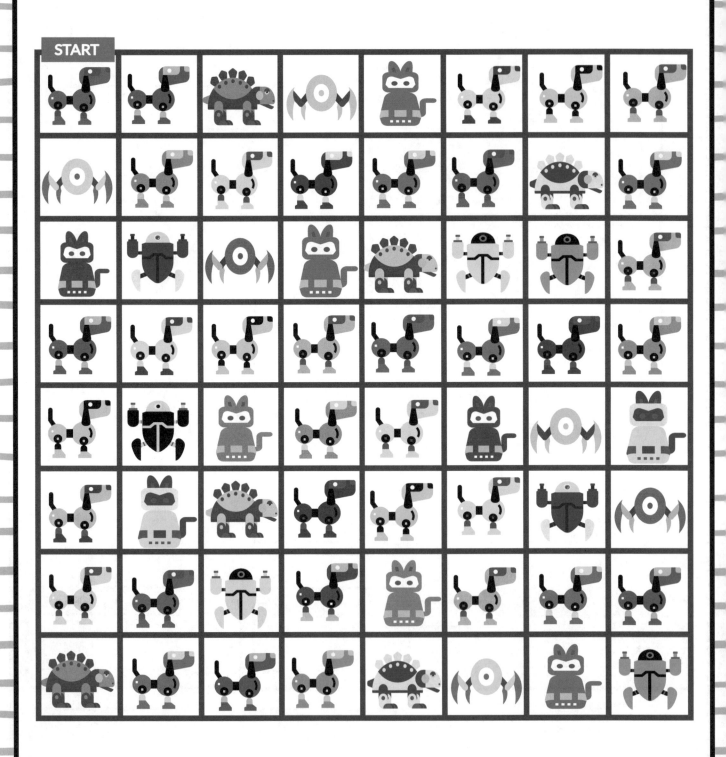

Gather all ROBO CATS without taking the pen off the paper.

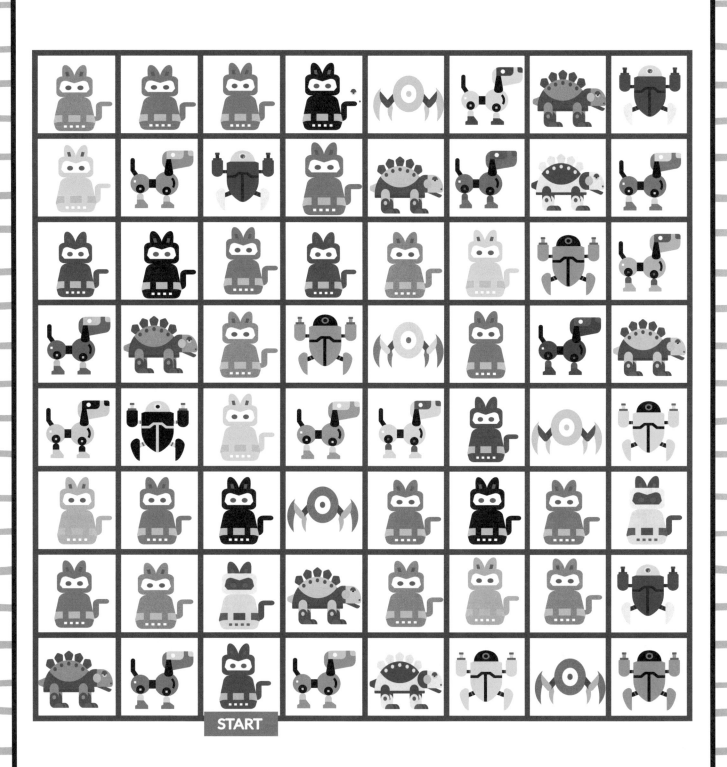

START

ACTIVITY 40

Sudoku 4x4. Draw the proper shapes in empty spaces.
Remember each row, each column, and each box may contain one
and only one of the possible shapes.

①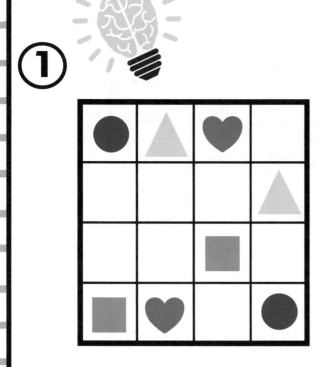

②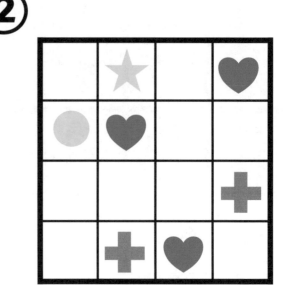

③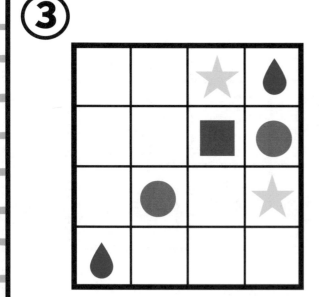

④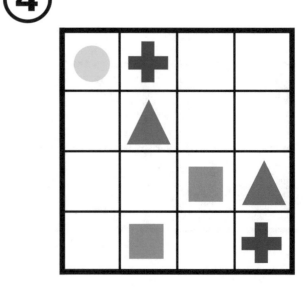

ACTIVITY 4

Sudoku 4x4. Write the proper numbers (1-4) in empty spaces.
Remember each row, each column, and each box may contain one
and only one of the possible numbers.

①

1			4
	4	3	
	2	1	
3			2

②

4		3	
	1		2
1		2	
	3		

③

4			1
1		3	
	4		3
3			2

④

1		4	2
4			
			4
2	4		3

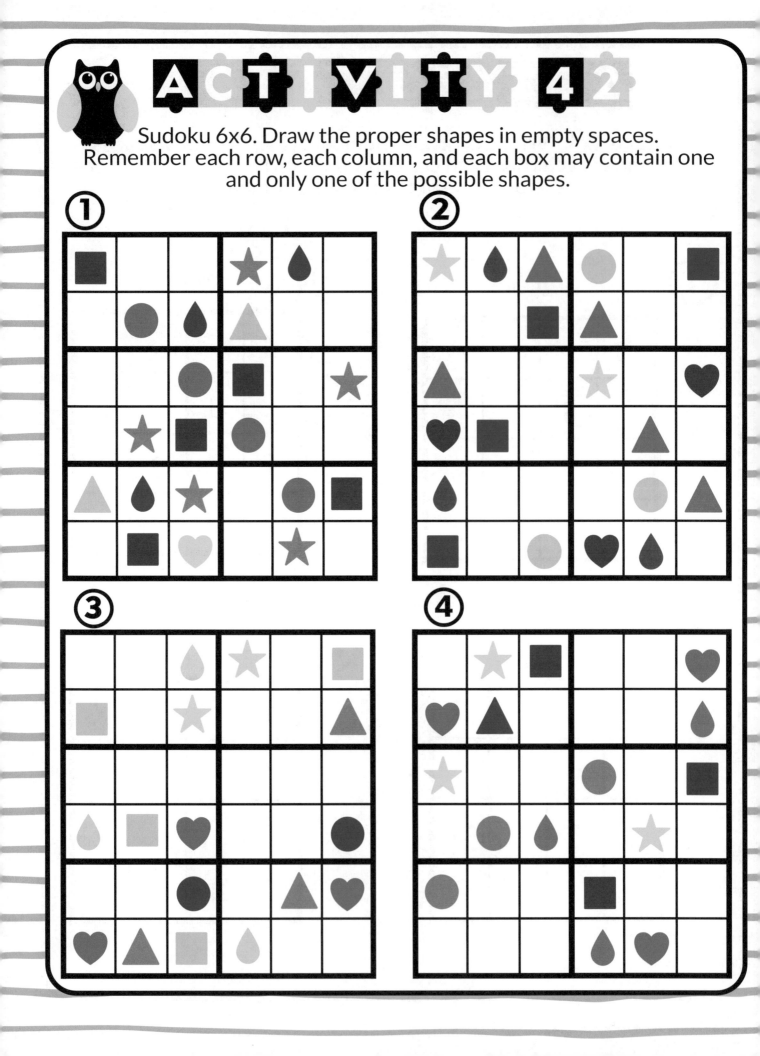

ACTIVITY 42

Sudoku 6x6. Draw the proper shapes in empty spaces.
Remember each row, each column, and each box may contain one
and only one of the possible shapes.

Sudoku 6x6. Write the proper numbers (1-6) in empty spaces. Remember each row, each column, and each box may contain one and only one of the possible numbers.

①

	6	4	3		2
			1		6
2		6	4	1	3
4	3		2	6	
	4	3			1
			5		

②

3	5	6	4	2	1
4			3		
	4	3	5	1	2
5	2	1		3	
2					
	6	4		5	

③

4		6		2	1
3	2	1		6	5
6		5			4
2				5	6
1	6		5	4	3
5	3			1	

④

2		5	3		1
1		3	2	5	
3	2	6	5		4
4		1		2	3
5	3		1	6	2
				3	5

ACTIVITY 44

Sudoku 9x9. Draw the proper shapes in empty spaces.
Remember each row, each column, and each box may contain one
and only one of the possible shapes.

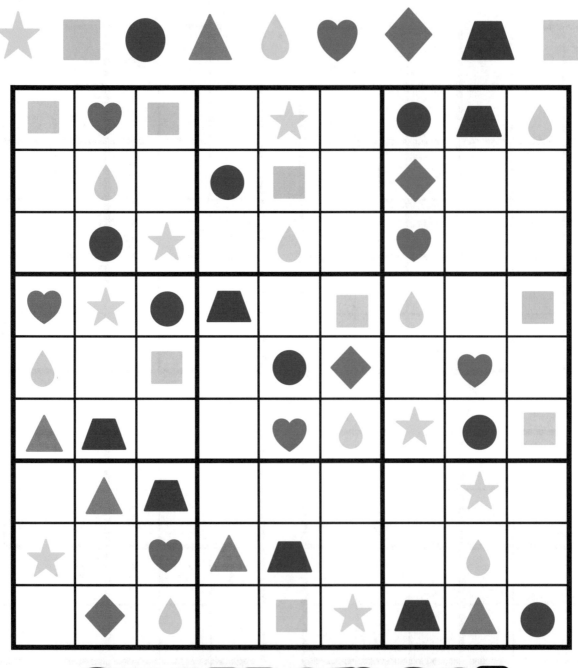

CHALLENGE!

Sudoku 9x9. Write the proper numbers (1-9) in empty spaces. Remember each row, each column, and each box may contain one and only one of the possible numbers.

CHALLENGE!

6	9	5	2		3	8	1	
7	2		6		8	3	9	5
	3	8	9	5	4		7	
	4		3		5	7	8	
3	8	7	4		2	9		1
		9			7		4	3
9			8	4		5		
	5	3	7				6	8
8	7			2	1	4	2	

Days of the week. Complete the table with the proper day of the week using the instructions below.

1: day of the week + 2
2: day of the week + 3
3: day of the week + 4
4: day of the week - 1
5: day of the week - 2

	MONDAY	TUESDAY	WEDNESDAY	THURSDAY	FRIDAY	SATURDAY	SUNDAY
1		MONDAY	WEDNESDAY				
2		SUNDAY			TUESDAY		
3		TUESDAY		WEDNESDAY			
4		FRIDAY			TUESDAY		
5		MONDAY					

ACTIVITY 47

Months. Complete the table with the proper month using the instructions below.

1: month + 2
2: month + 3
3: month + 4
4: month - 1
5: month - 3

JANUARY MARCH MAY JULY SEPTEMBER NOVEMBER
FEBRUARY APRIL JUNE AUGUST OCTOBER DECEMBER

1	JANUARY	MARCH			
2	MARCH			DECEMBER	
3	FEBRUARY				JUNE
4	SEPTEMBER			JUNE	
5	DECEMBER				

Maths logic challenge.
Use your math skills to decode the value of each robot.

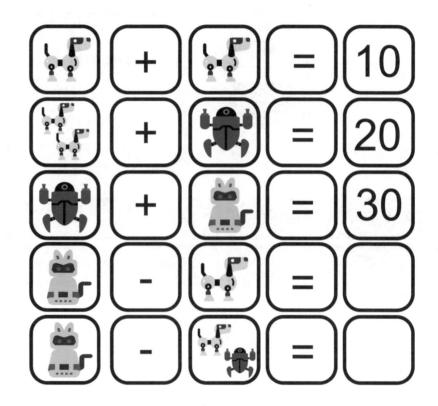

Maths logic challenge.
Solve the last equation.

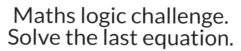
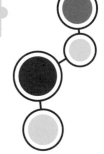

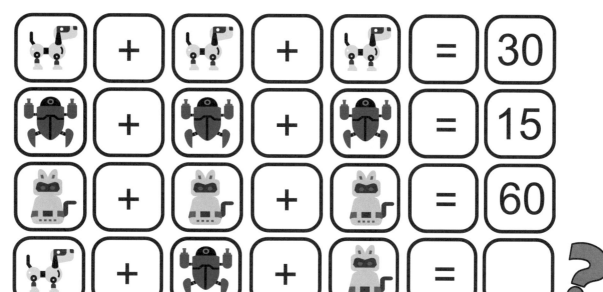

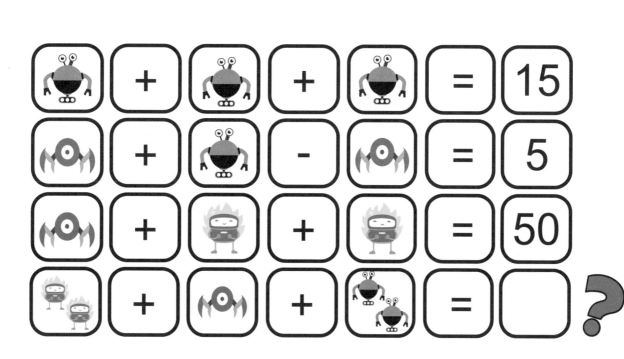

MYSTERY NUMBER - maths logic challenge.
Use the key to find out what the mystery numbers are.
Write the numbers in the boxes.

example:

5 ↑ ↑ ← [20]

5 +10 +10 -5 = 20

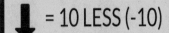

KEY:

↑ = 10 MORE (+10)

↓ = 10 LESS (-10)

→ = 5 MORE (+5)

← = 5 LESS (-5)

① 10 ↑ ↑ ↓ ☐

----

② 5 → → ← ← ☐

----

③ 10 ← ↑ ← → ☐

----

④ 1 → ↑ ← → ☐

----

⑤ 20 ↓ ← ← ☐

----

⑥ 15 → ← ← ☐

----

⑦ 5 ← ↑ ← ↑ → ☐

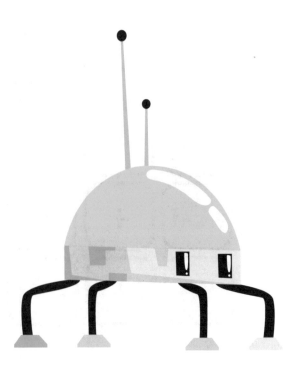

ACTIVITY 51

MYSTERY NUMBER - maths logic challenge.
Use the key to find out what the mystery numbers are.
Write the numbers in the boxes.

example:

5 ↑ ↑ ← 35

5 +20 +20 -10 = 35

① 10 ↑ ↑ ↑ ☐

② 15 ↑ → ↑ ← ☐

③ 7 → ↑ ← ↓ ☐

④ 20 → ↓ → → ☐

⑤ 25 ↑ ↑ ← ← ↓ ☐

⑥ 17 → ↑ ↑ → ↓ ☐

⑦ 35 ↓ → → ↑ ← ☐

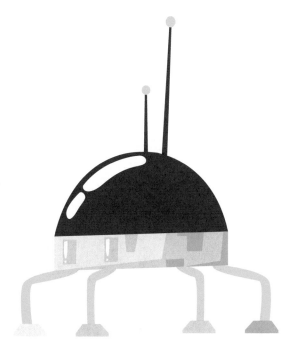

BINARY CODE is a system that is based only
on two numbers, „0" and „1".
This code is used in computers.
Everything you see on the computer: letters, numbers, pictures
is made up of a different combination of two numbers: „0" and „1".

Convert the images into binary code. Use „0" to represent
a clear pixel/box and „1" to represent a filled pixel/box.

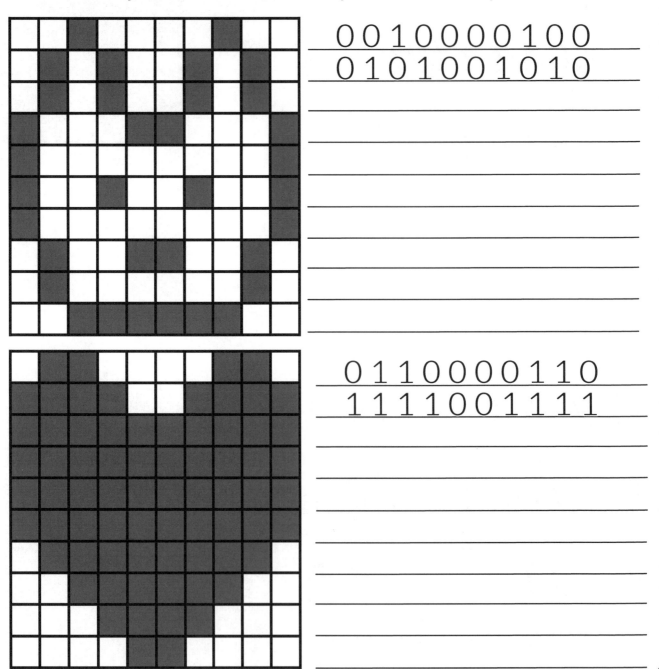

0010000100
0101001010

0110000110
1111001111

A C T I V I T Y 5 3

Convert the binary codes into images. Leave all „0" pixels/boxes
clear and color all pixels/boxes that have the value „1".

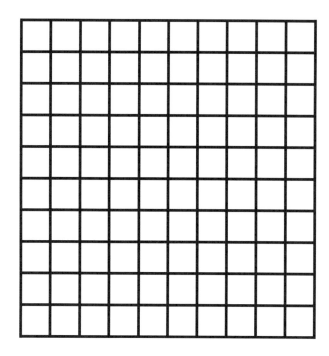

```
0 0 1 1 1 1 1 1 0 0
0 1 0 0 0 0 0 0 1 0
1 0 0 0 0 0 0 0 0 1
1 0 1 0 0 0 0 1 0 1
1 0 1 0 0 0 0 1 0 1
1 0 0 0 0 0 0 0 0 1
1 0 1 0 0 0 0 1 0 1
1 0 0 1 1 1 1 0 0 1
0 1 0 0 0 0 0 0 1 0
0 0 1 1 1 1 1 1 0 0
```

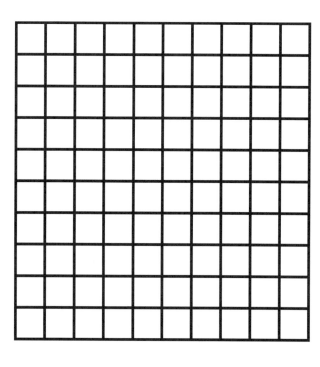

```
0 0 0 1 1 1 1 0 0 0
0 0 0 1 1 1 1 0 0 0
0 0 1 0 0 0 0 1 0 0
0 1 0 0 1 0 0 0 1 0
0 1 0 0 1 0 0 0 1 0
0 1 0 0 1 1 1 0 1 0
0 1 0 0 0 0 0 0 1 0
0 0 1 0 0 0 0 1 0 0
0 0 0 1 1 1 1 0 0 0
0 0 0 1 1 1 1 0 0 0
```

ACTIVITY 54

LETTERS OF THE ALPHABET IN BINARY CODE.

A 01000001	B 01000010	C 01000011	D 01000100	E 01000101	F 01000110
G 01000111	H 01001000	I 01001001	J 01001010	K 01001011	L 01001100
M 01001101	N 01001110	O 01001111	P 01010000	Q 01010001	R 01010010
S 01010011	T 01010100	U 01010101	V 01010110	W 01010111	X 01011000
		Y 01011001	Z 1011010		

Write the binary code for each word.

H	01001000
E	
L	
L	
O	

W	
O	
R	
L	
D	

S	
M	
I	
L	
E	

ACTIVITY 55

Write the binary code for each letter.
Then fill in the squares that equal „1".

I AM:

F	01000110	☐■■☐☐☐■■☐
U		
N		
N		
Y		

B		
R		
A		
V		
E		

J		
O		
Y		
F		
U		
L		

Crack the binary code.

Letter	Binary
A	01000001
B	01000010
C	01000011
D	01000100
E	01000101
F	01000110
G	01000111
H	01001000
I	01001001
J	01001010
K	01001011
L	01001100
M	01001101
N	01001110
O	01001111
P	01010000
Q	01010001
R	01010010
S	01010011
T	01010100
U	01010101
V	01010110
W	01010111
X	01011000
Y	01011001
Z	1011010

Y   **O**
01011001   01001111   01010101   01000001   01010010   01000101

01010011   01010101   01000011   01001000   01000001

01000111   01010010   01000101   01000001   01010100

01001011   01001001   01000100

01000100   01010010   01000101   01000001   01001101

01000010   01001001   01000111

01001110   01000101   01010110   01000101   01010010

01000111   01001001   01010110   01000101

01010101   01010000

ACTIVITY 57

In the space below, write you name
or anything you want in the binary code.

_____

_____

_____

_____

_____

_____

_____

_____

_____

_____

ACTIVITY 58

Repeat the patterns. Draw by squares.

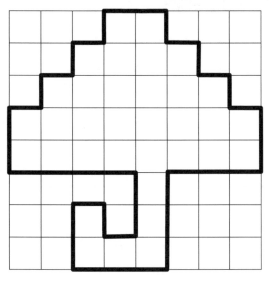

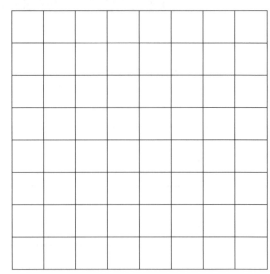

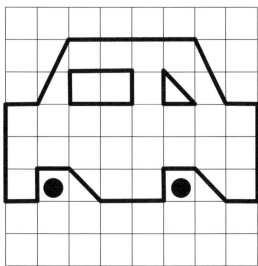

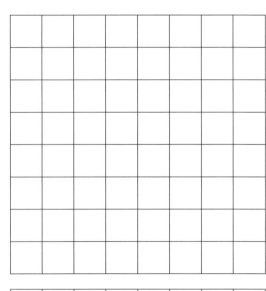

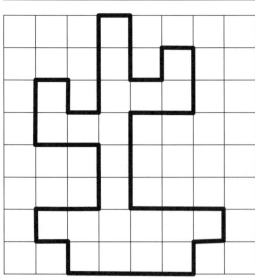

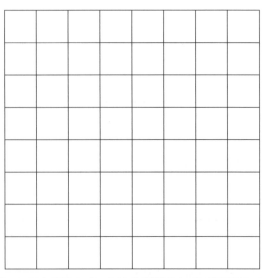

ACTIVITY 59

Repeat the patterns. Join the dots.

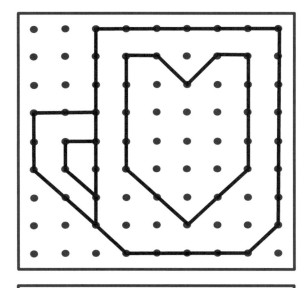
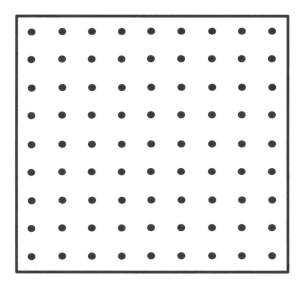

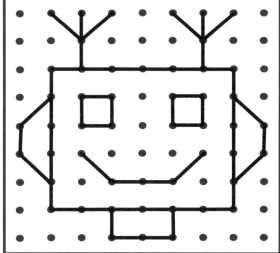
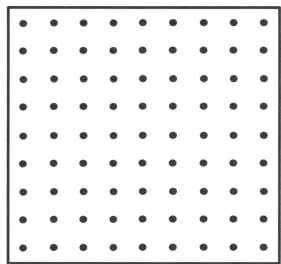

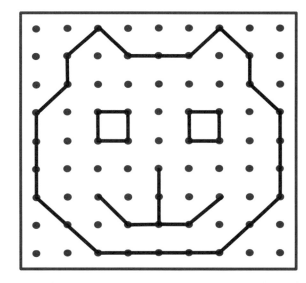
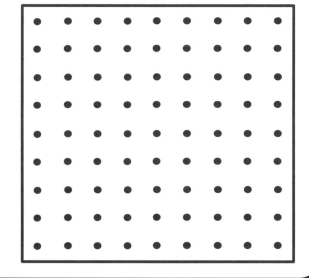

ACTIVITY 60

Connect the dots by following the code. Start from the red dot.

↑ → → ↓ ↓ ← ← ↑

→ ↓ → ↓ → ↓ → ↓

→ ↑ → ↓ → ↑ → ↓

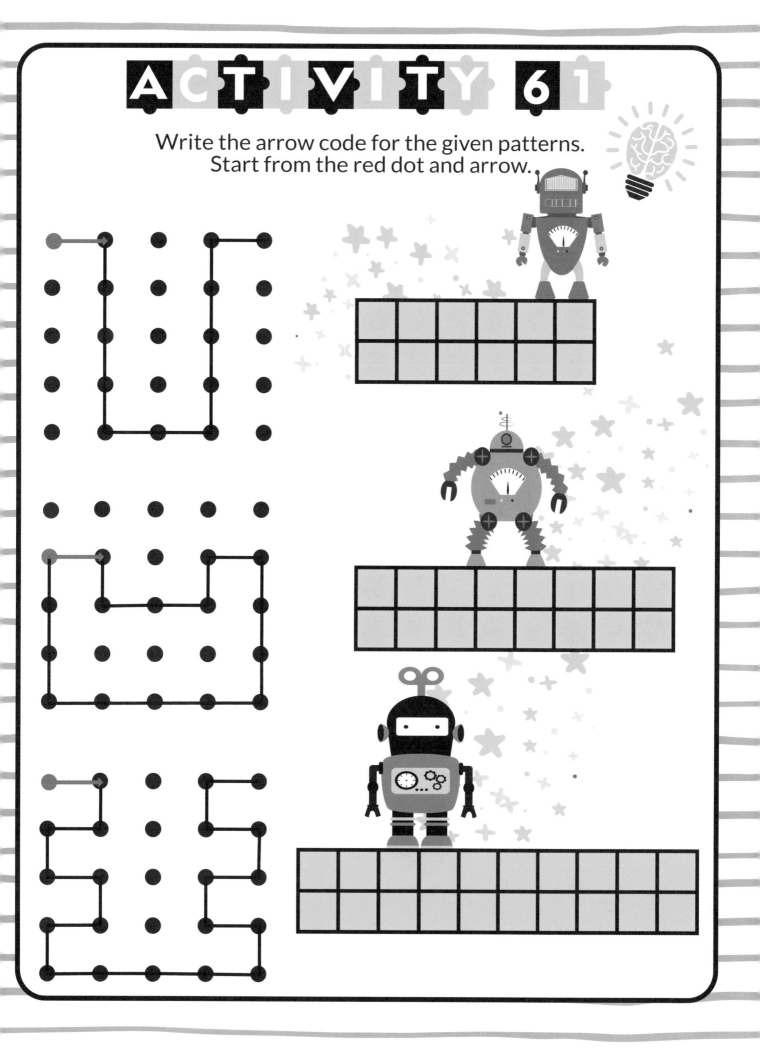

ACTIVITY 62

Draw by code. Start from the red dot.

•	1 →	1 ↑	1 →	1 ↑	2 →	1 ↑
	1 →	1 ↗	2 →	1 ↓	1 ✓	2 →
	1 ↓	1 →	3 ↗	3 ↓	1 ✓	1 ↘
	3 ↓	3 ↘	1 ↓	1 ←	1 ↓	2 ←
	1 ↘	1 ↓	2 ←	1 ↘	1 ←	1 ↑
	2 ←	1 ↑	1 ←	1 ↑	1 ←	1 ↑

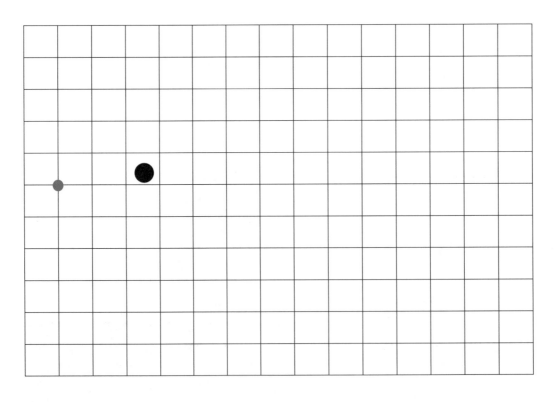

ACTIVITY 63

Draw by code. Start from the red dot.

●	1	↗	1	↘	1	↑	1	↗	1	→	1	↘
	1	↓	1	↙	1	↘	5	↗	1	↘	5	↓
	1	↙	1	↘	3	↓	2	↙	2	←	2	↘
	1	↓	1	↙	1	←	1	↘	1	↑	2	↙
	2	←	2	↘	3	↑	1	↗	1	↘	5	↑
	1	↗	5	↘								

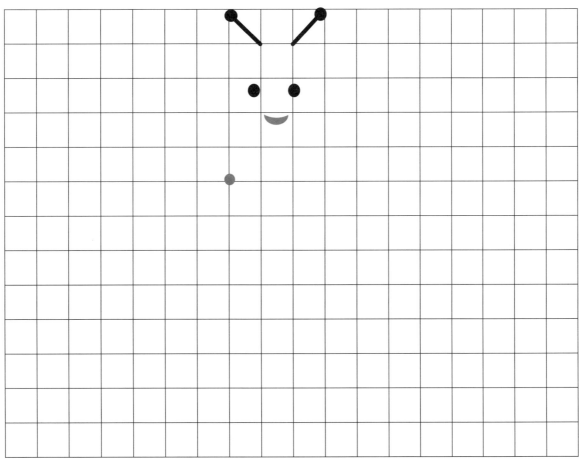

Draw by code. Start from the red dot.

•	7 →	5 ↘	4 ↓	1 ↙	1 ↘	1 ↑
	1 ↘	2 ↑	1 ↘	7 ↓	1 ←	1 ↓
	1 ←	1 ↙	3 ←	1 ↘	1 ←	1 ↑
	1 ←	7 ↑	1 ↙	2 ↓	1 ↙	1 ↓
	1 ↙	1 ↘	4 ↑	5 ↗		

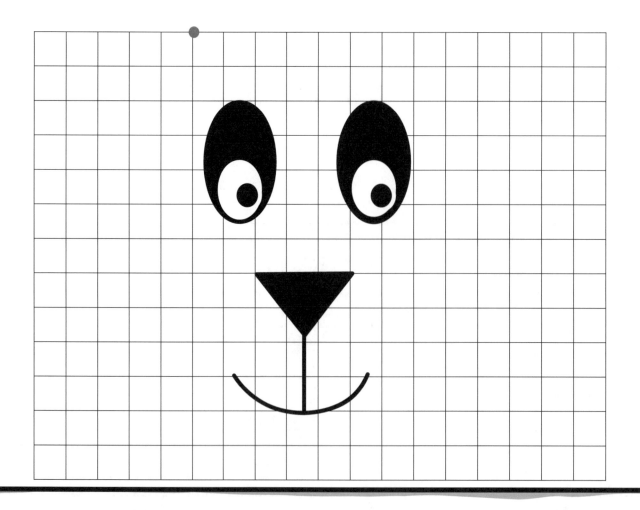

Draw by code. Start from the red dot.

●	1	↘	1	↑	1	↗	1	→	1	↙	1	↘
	4	→	1	↗	1	↘	1	→	1	↘	1	↓
	1	↙	2	↓	2	→	1	↘	1	↓	1	↙
	2	↑	2	←	2	↓	1	↙	2	↓	1	→
	1	↘	3	←	3	↑	2	←	3	↓	3	←
	1	↗	1	→	2	↑	1	↘	2	↑	2	←
	2	↓	1	↘	1	↑	1	↗	2	→	2	↑

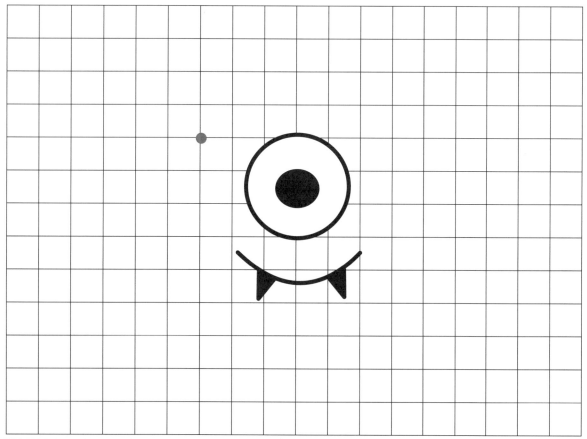

What are the secret words? Follow the code to find out.

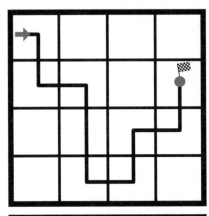

B	A	P	D
U	T	G	Y
S	T	F	L
H	E	R	Z

_____

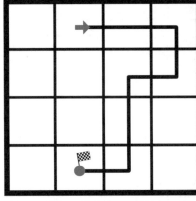

Z	L	A	D
R	T	B	Y
S	R	I	L
B	D	R	F

_____

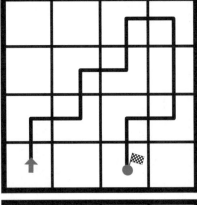

D	V	H	O
L	S	S	P
R	A	E	P
G	T	R	K

_____

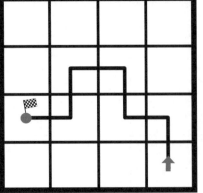

B	D	C	F
O	F	E	S
Y	L	R	I
A	E	P	F

_____

What are the secret sentences? Follow the code to find out.

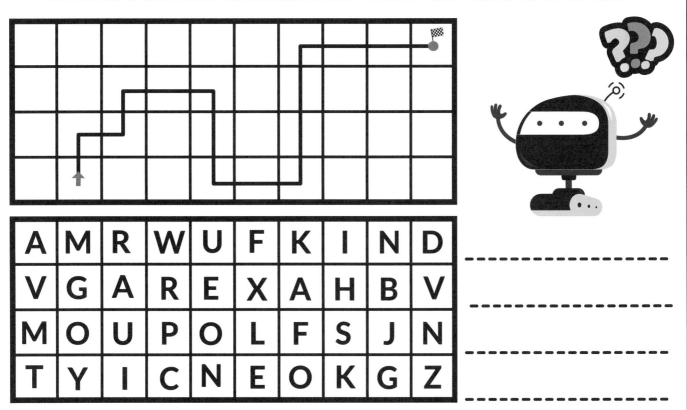

A	M	R	W	U	F	K	I	N	D
V	G	A	R	E	X	A	H	B	V
M	O	U	P	O	L	F	S	J	N
T	Y	I	C	N	E	O	K	G	Z

F	O	Y	I	C	N	D	O	K	G
N	L	L	Y	O	A	E	P	F	U
P	V	O	W	U	R	E	G	J	B
T	X	A	Z	R	D	A	M	S	Q

What are the secret words? Follow the arrow code to find out.

R	A	S	D
A	I	N	B
S	H	F	O
T	G	R	W

R _____

A	E	A	F
R	Y	J	Y
N	I	C	N
U	V	O	R

U _____

B	J	A	U
D	I	S	R
G	N	O	P
N	E	R	Q

D _____

G	M	C	U
A	O	N	Z
B	T	S	I
J	E	R	L

M _____

What are the secret sentences? Follow the arrow code to find out.

F	P	K	Q	C	V	S	A	L	C
G	L	L	Y	O	E	C	I	F	M
Y	O	I	E	S	P	E	G	E	K
T	U	A	R	N	D	B	H	S	Q

Y _____

T	H	E	R	E	D	S	Y	L	I
G	L	W	Y	E	E	C	O	U	P
Y	T	O	R	N	P	D	G	N	K
F	U	A	L	D	M	K	J	H	Q

T _____

W	Y	E	Q	E	N	G	K	S	A
F	O	U	T	E	O	E	O	A	Y
J	T	G	E	T	R	R	G	D	Y
M	U	D	N	S	T	E	V	E	R

Y _____

_____

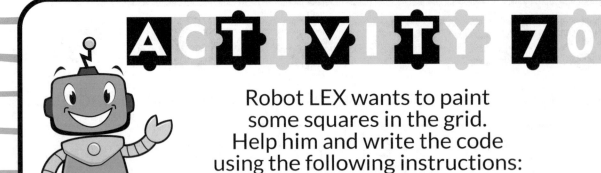

Robot LEX wants to paint
some squares in the grid.
Help him and write the code
using the following instructions:

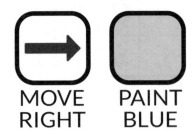

MOVE
RIGHT

PAINT
BLUE

example:

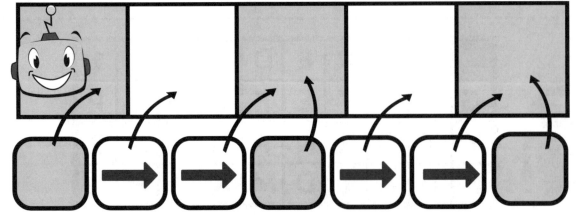

First, Robot Lex paints the square in blue. Next, he has to make
two moves right to paint the next square in blue.
Then, he moves right twice and paints the last square in blue.

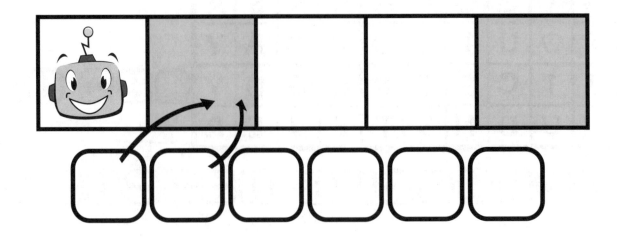

Robot LEX wants to paint some squares in the grid. Help him and write the code using the following instructions:

 MOVE RIGHT

 PAINT BLUE

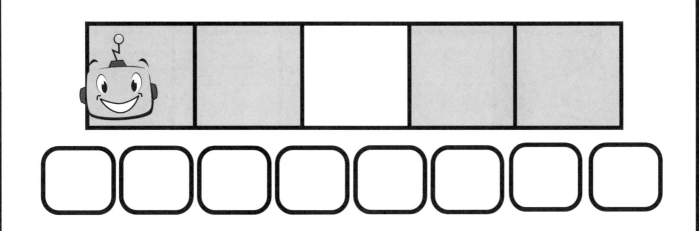

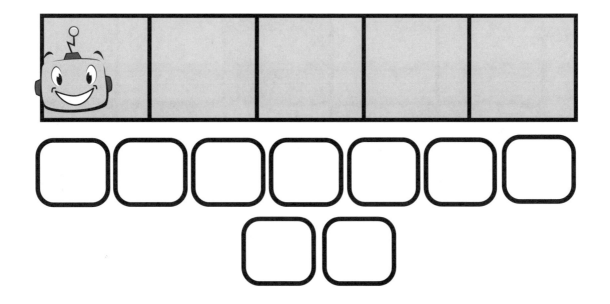

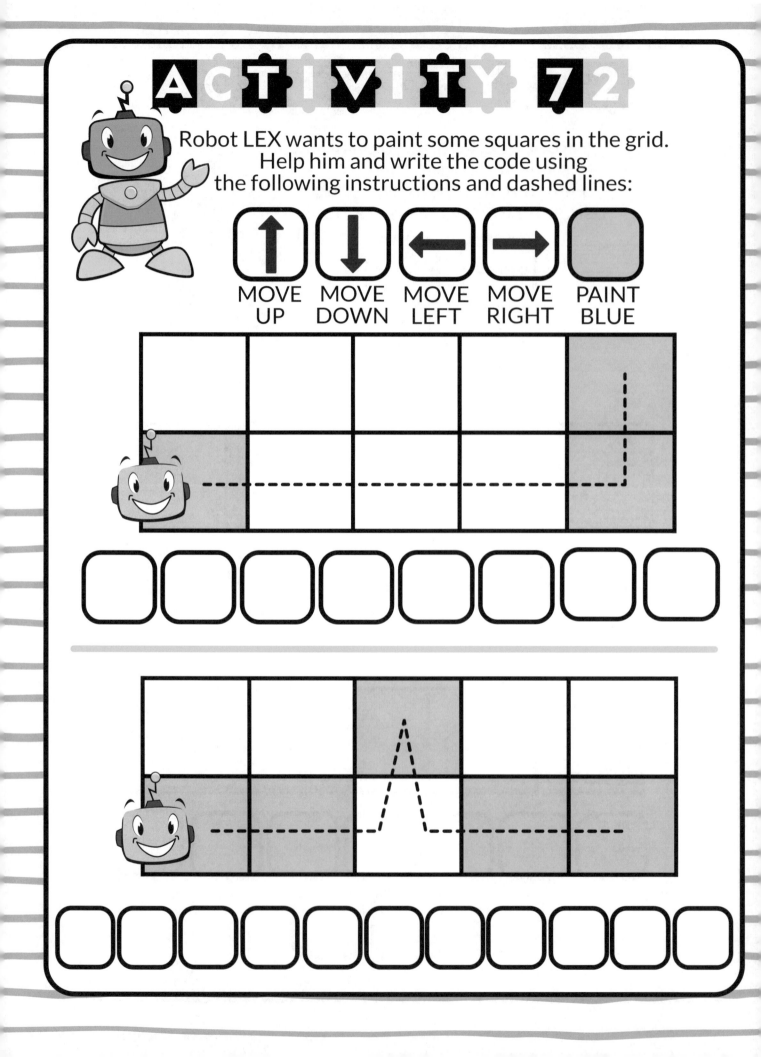

ACTIVITY 73

Robot LEX wants to paint some squares in the grid.
Help him and write the code using
the following instructions and dashed lines:

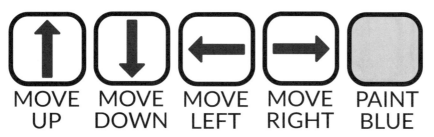

| MOVE UP | MOVE DOWN | MOVE LEFT | MOVE RIGHT | PAINT BLUE |

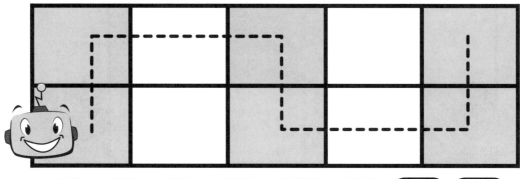

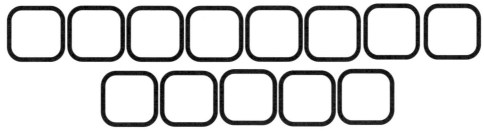

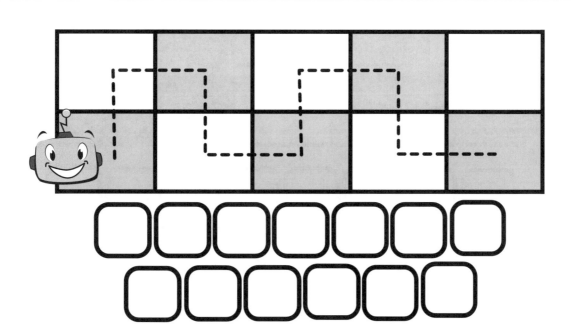

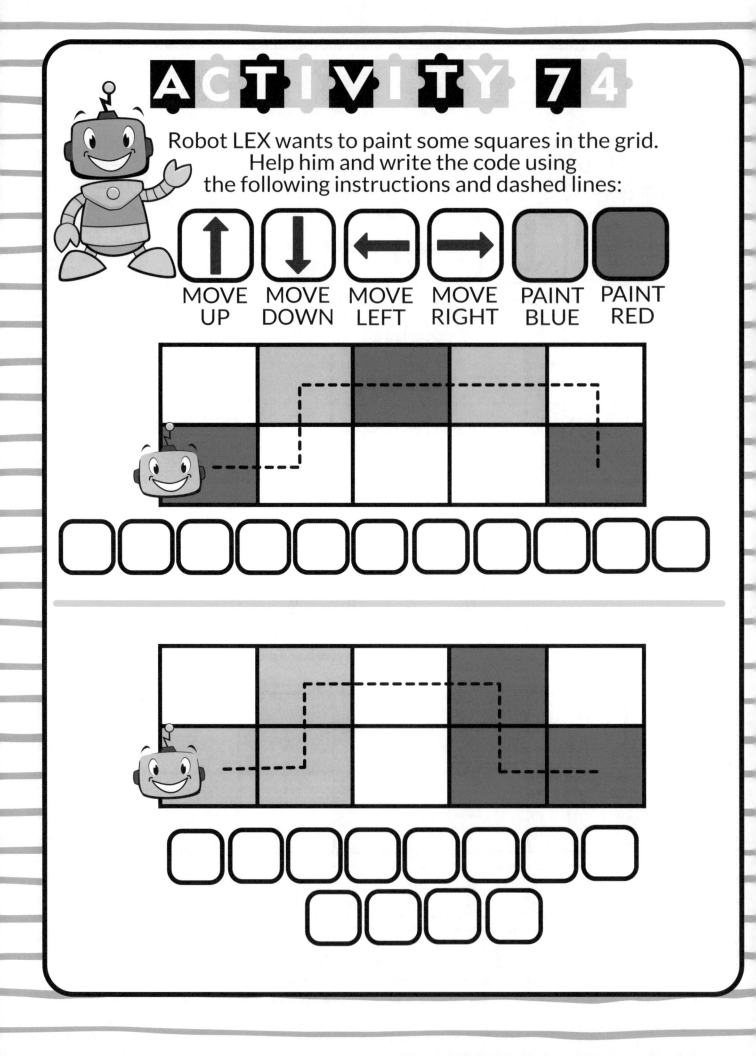

ACTIVITY 74

Robot LEX wants to paint some squares in the grid.
Help him and write the code using
the following instructions and dashed lines:

MOVE UP | MOVE DOWN | MOVE LEFT | MOVE RIGHT | PAINT BLUE | PAINT RED

ACTIVITY 75

Robot LEX wants to paint some squares in the grid.
Help him and write the code using
the following instructions and dashed lines:

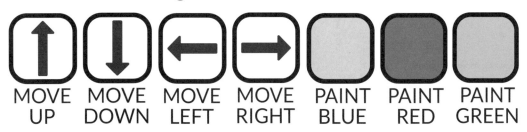

| MOVE UP | MOVE DOWN | MOVE LEFT | MOVE RIGHT | PAINT BLUE | PAINT RED | PAINT GREEN |

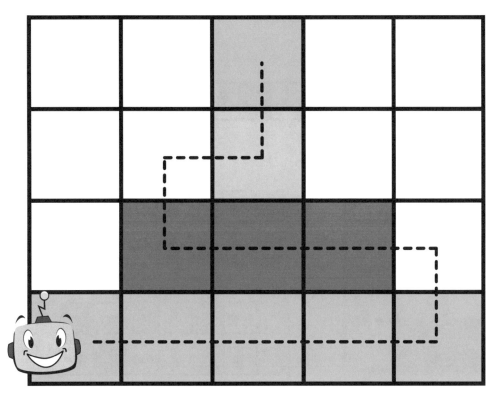

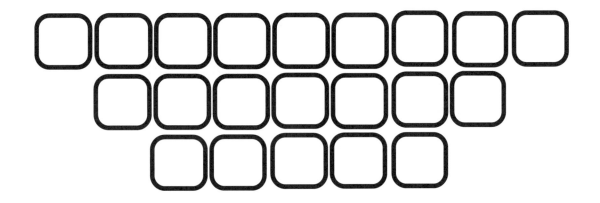

ACTIVITY 76

Which code is correct A or B?

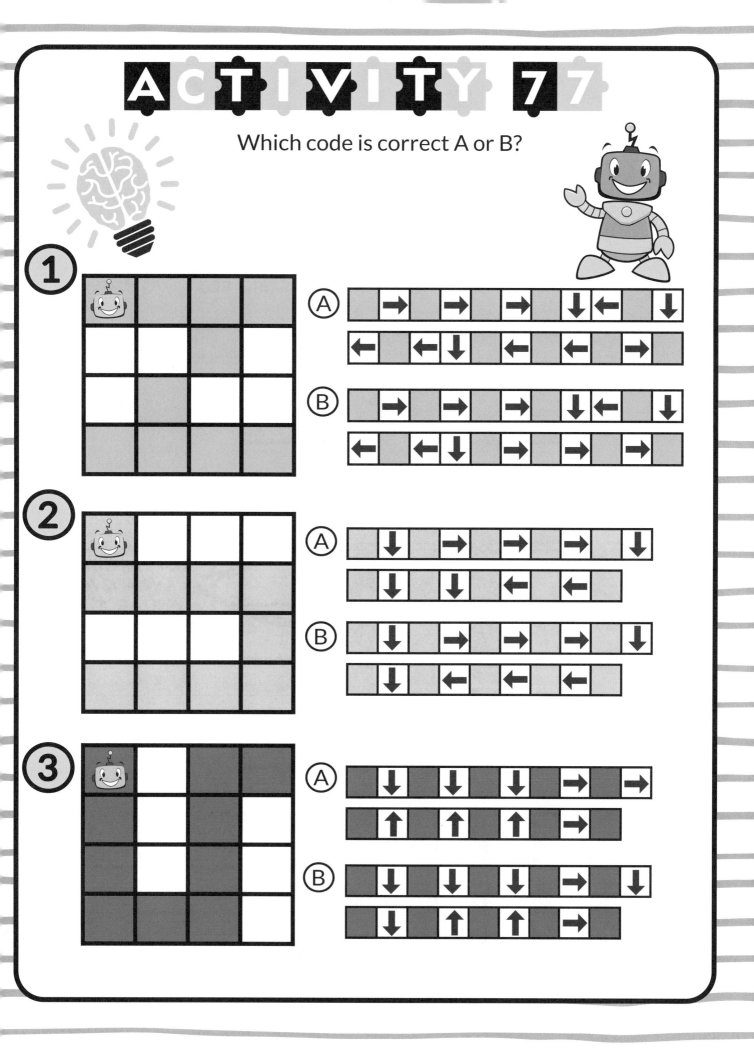

ACTIVITY 77

Which code is correct A or B?

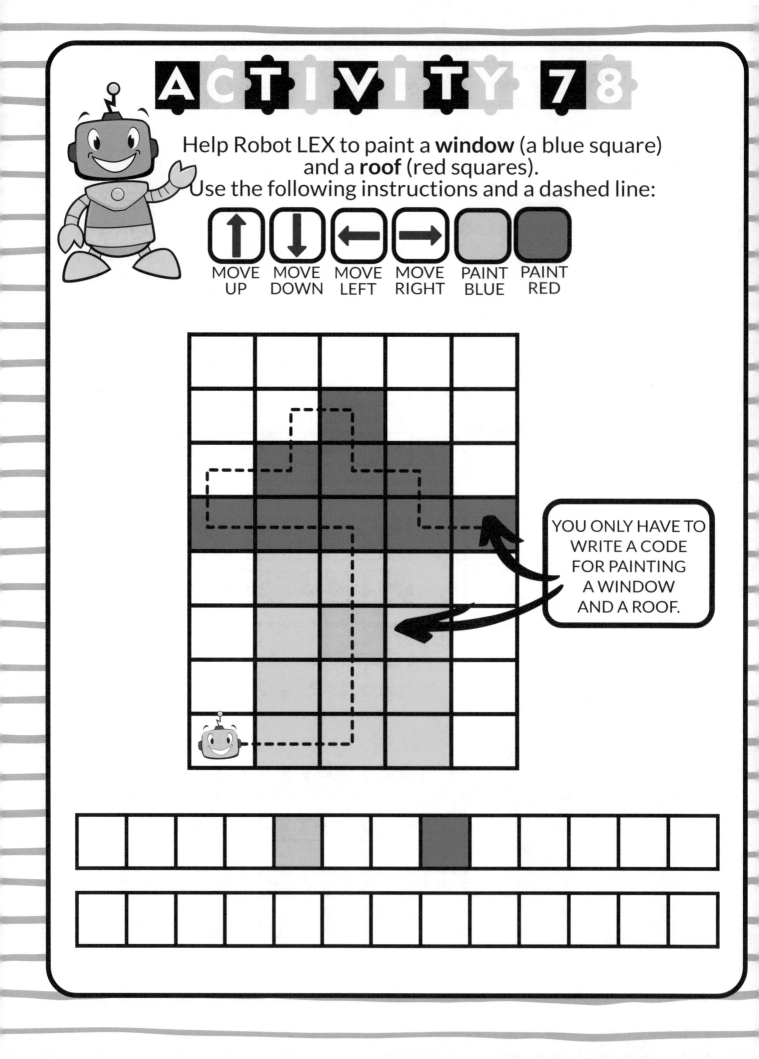

Help Robot LEX to paint a flower.
Use the following instructions and a dashed line:

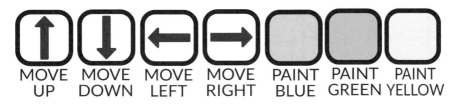

MOVE UP | MOVE DOWN | MOVE LEFT | MOVE RIGHT | PAINT BLUE | PAINT GREEN | PAINT YELLOW

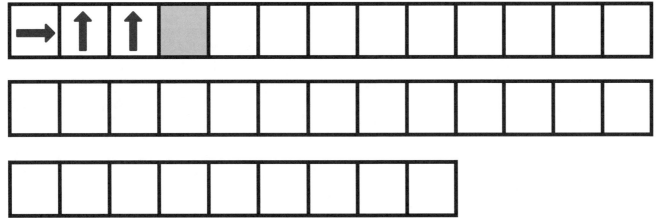

ACTIVITY 80

Help Robot LEO to paint the grids.
Use the codes to color the grids.

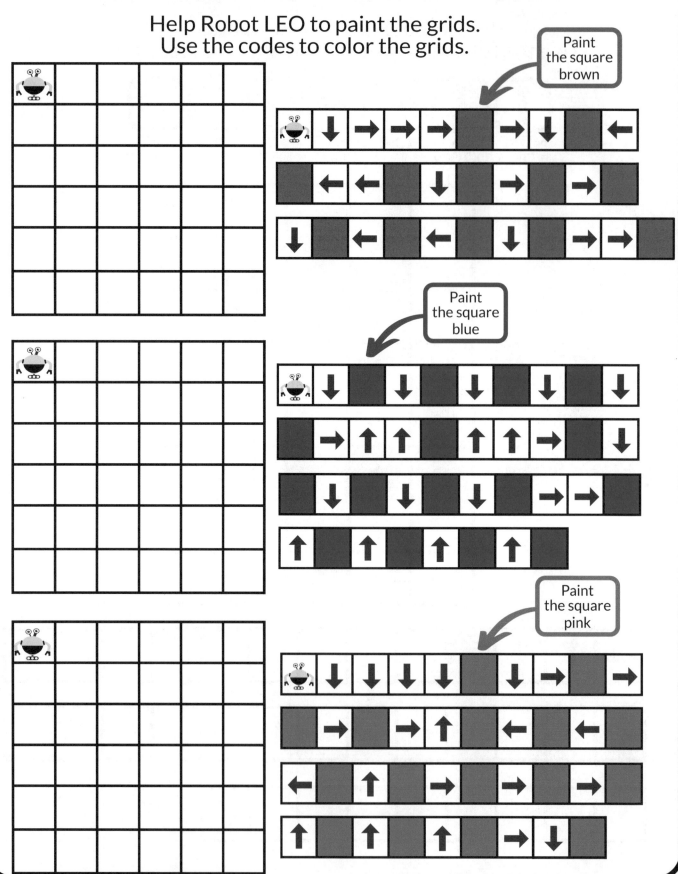

Paint the square brown

Paint the square blue

Paint the square pink

ACTIVITY 81

Help Robot LEO to paint the grids.
Use the codes to color the grids.

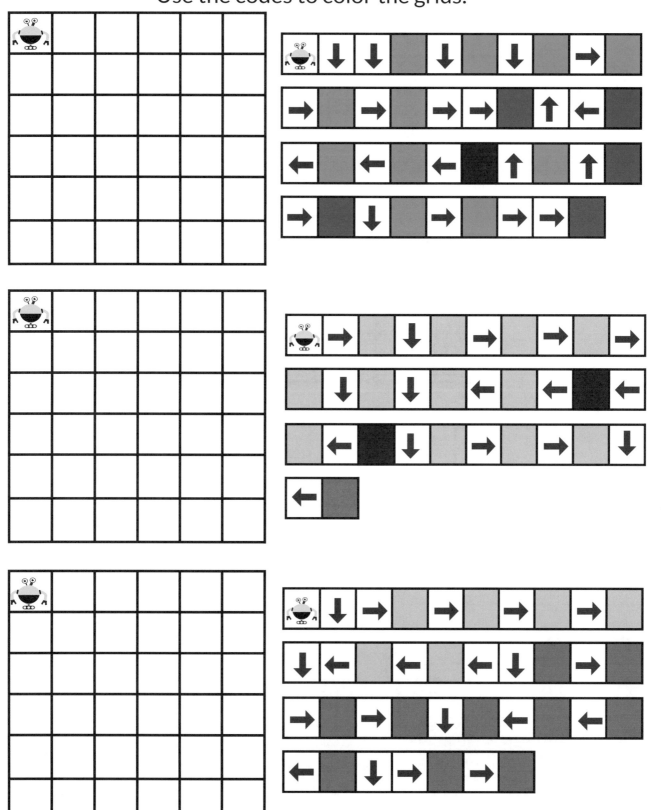

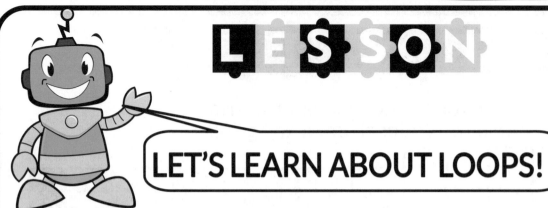

LESSON

LET'S LEARN ABOUT LOOPS!

LOOPS - are very useful in coding. Loops make your code shorter. Any time Robot Lex repeats the same task multiple times, he is looping an action.

example 1: Robot LEX wants to visit his friend Robot MAX.

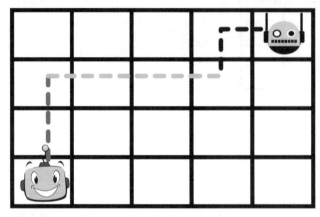

code without LOOPS:

This action / move is repeated twice.

This action / move is repeated three times.

These actions / moves are NOT repeated.

code with LOOPS:

In this square we write how many times the action is repeated.

These are LOOPS.

These actions / moves are NOT repeated so they are not in the loops.

example 2: Robot LEX wants to paint 5 squares in red and 5 squares in yellow.

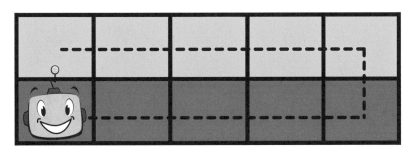

code without LOOPS:

The action of painting the squares and moving is repeated.

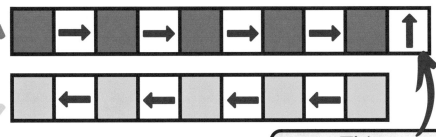

This mction / move is NOT repeated.

code with LOOPS:

This action is out of loop because it is a single action, not repeated.

In this square we write how many times the action is repeated.

These are LOOPS.

IT'S TIME YOU PRACTICED LOOPS!

ACTIVITY 82

Robot LEX wants to charge his battery.
Write the code with LOOPS.

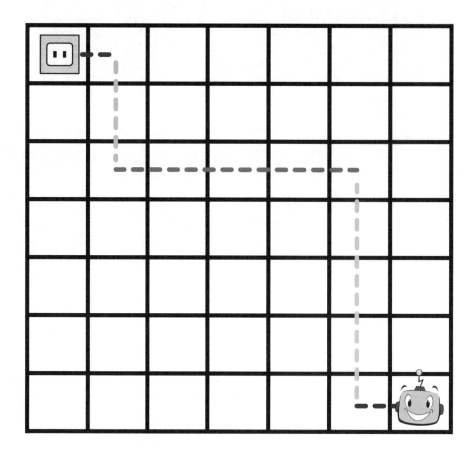

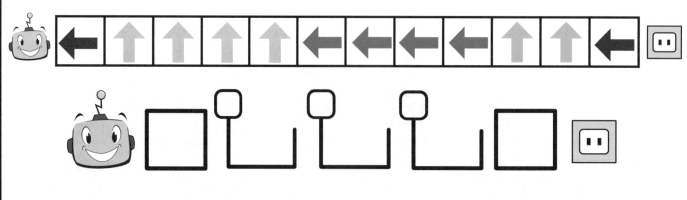

EXCELLENT!

ACTIVITY 83

Robot LEX loves flowers. Can you help him to pick them up?
Write the codes with LOOPS.

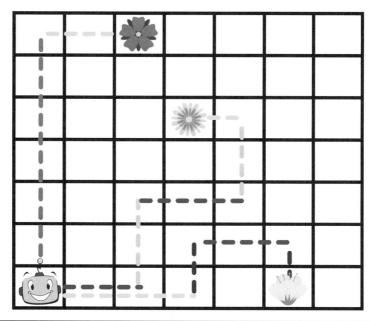

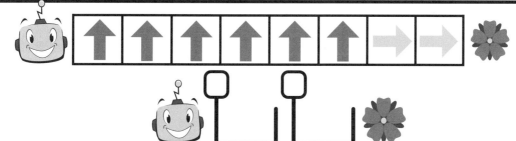

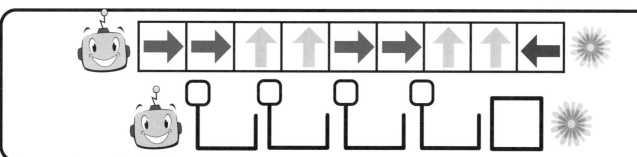

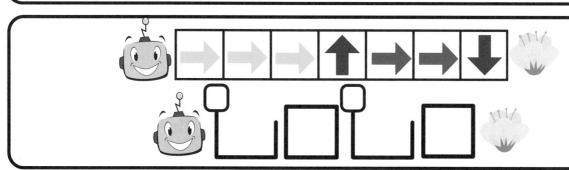

Robot LEX wants to tidy his room up. Help him pick up all his toys.
Write the arrow codes with and without LOOPS.

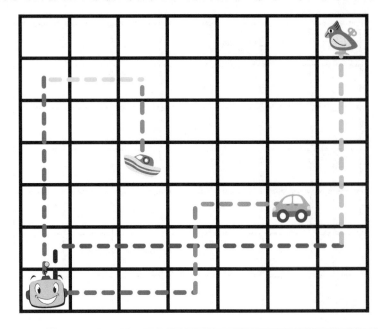

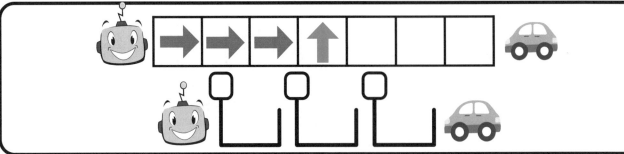

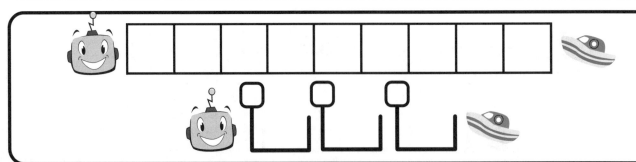

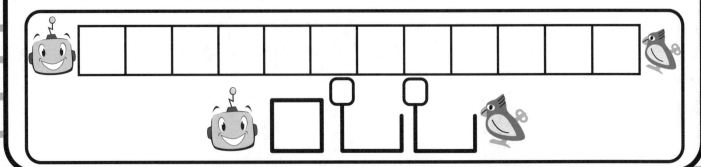

Help Robot LEX to get to his three friends.
Use the codes to draw him the routes.

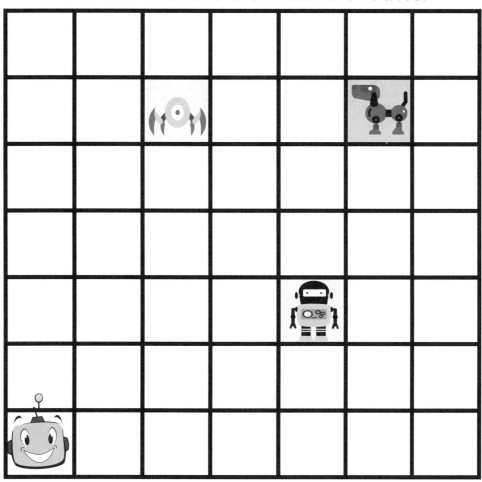

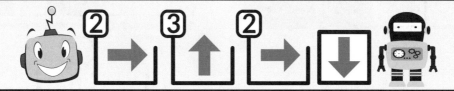

ACTIVITY 86

Robot LEX has already painted the grids.
Help him write the codes with LOOPS.

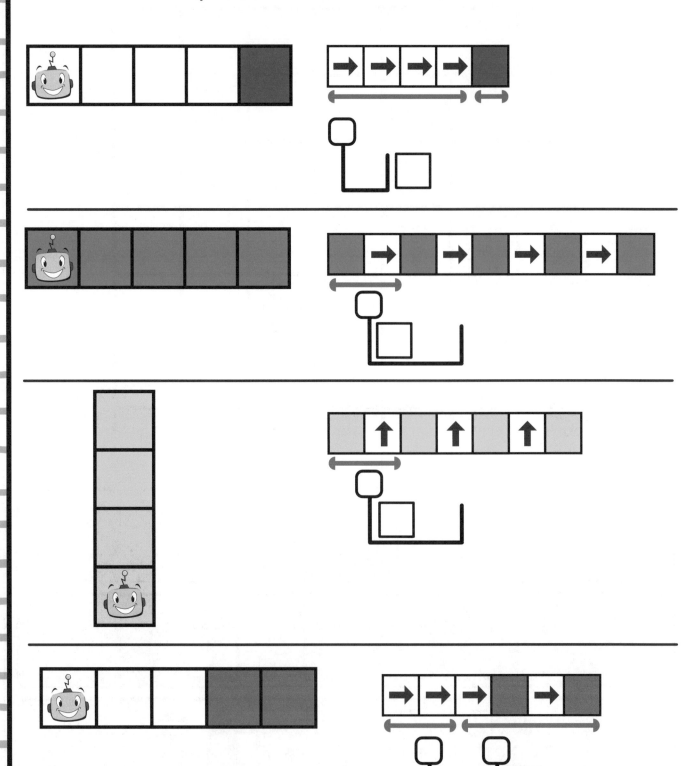

Robot LEX has already painted the grids.
Help him write the codes with LOOPS.

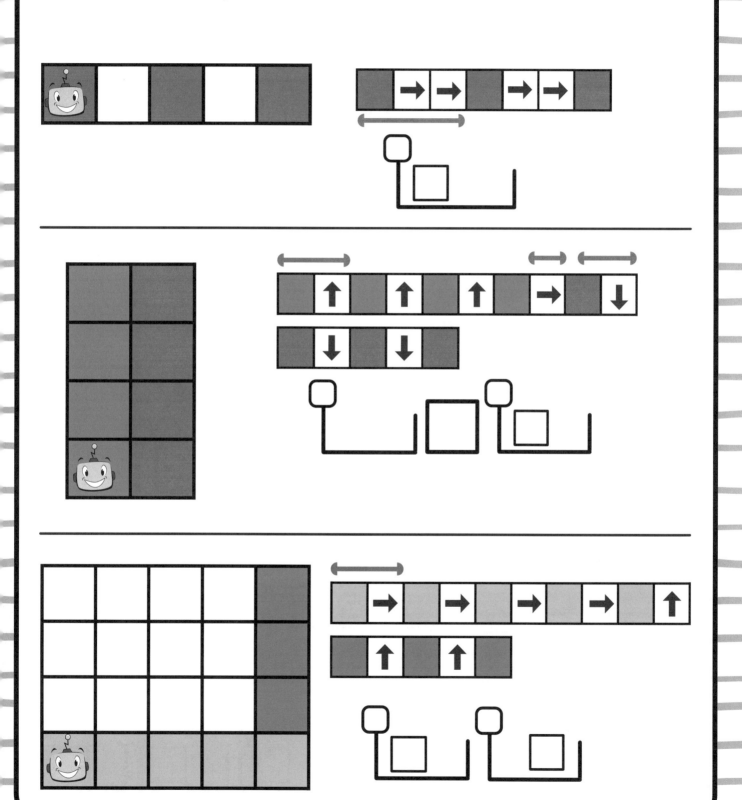

ACTIVITY 8

Robot LEX has already painted the grids.
Help him write the codes with LOOPS.

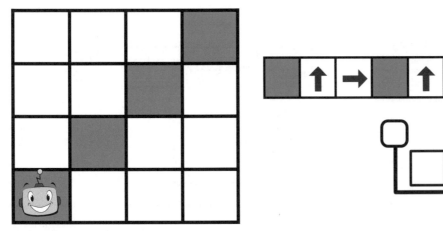

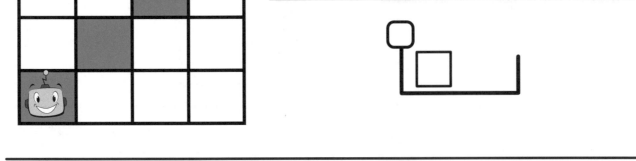

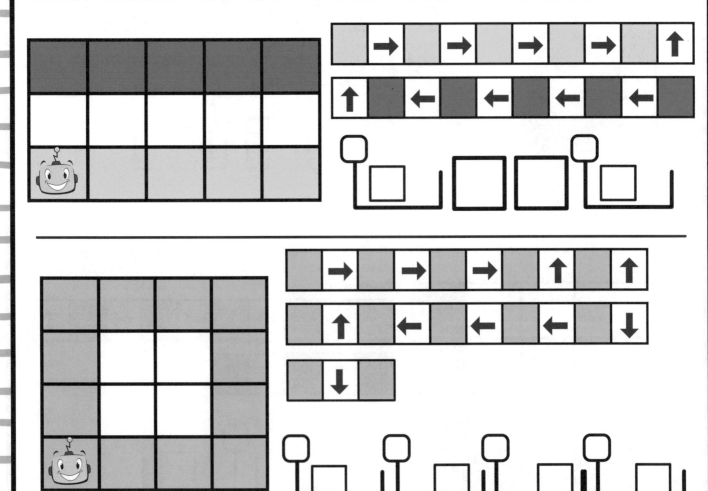

Robot LEX has already painted the grids.
Help him write the codes with LOOPS.

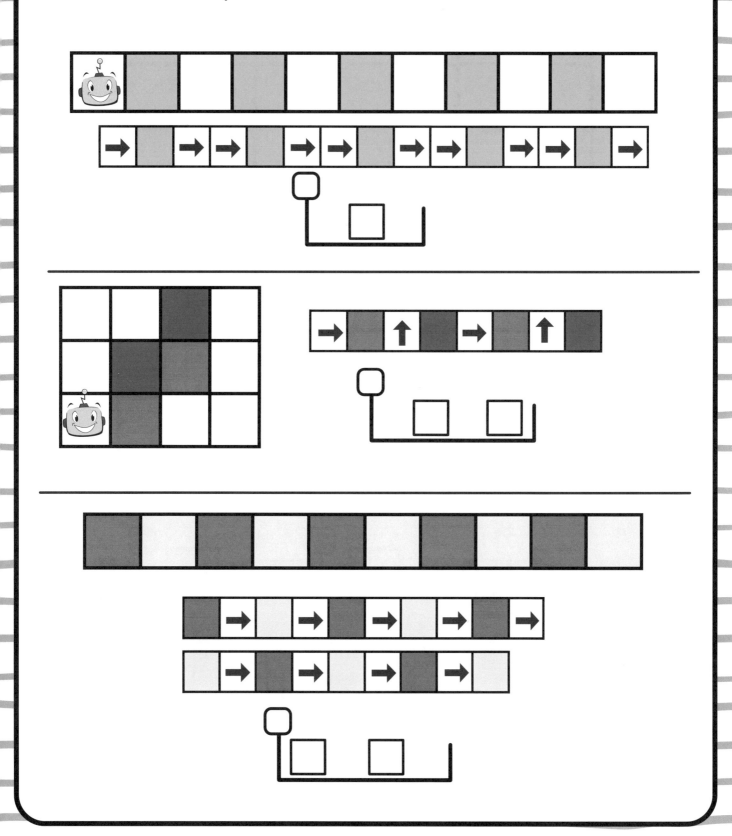

ACTIVITY 90

Help Robot LEX paint the grid by following the code.

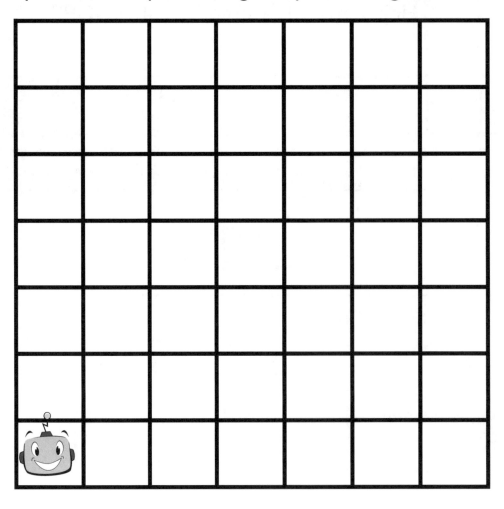

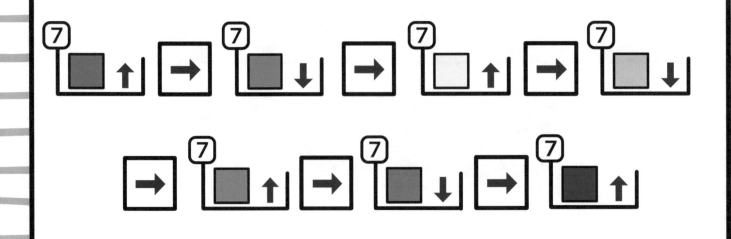

ACTIVITY 91

Cut out the Robots and color them.

Meet Robot ARCHIE.
Archie can:

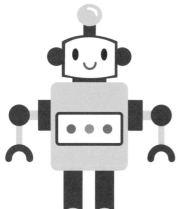

F move forward

↰ turn left

↱ turn right

Help Robot Archie to get to the playground.
Write the codes using:

F **↰** **↱**

example:

CODE:

F **↱** **F** **↰** **F**

START

It's your turn now!

CODE:

☐ ☐ ☐ ☐ ☐

START

ACTIVITY 9

Help Robot Archie to get to the playground.
Write the codes using:

CODE:

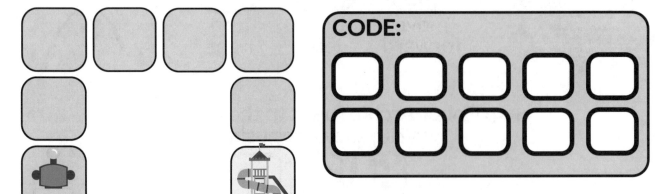

This time I want
to pick up some flowers on my way
to the playground.
Write the code using:

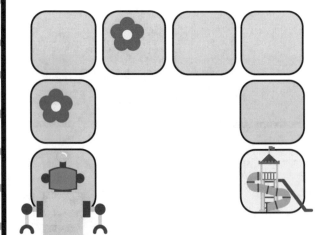

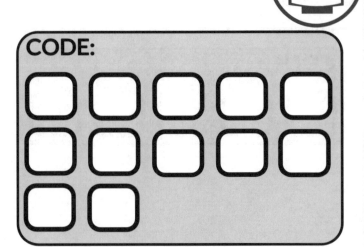

CODE:

ACTIVITY 94

Help Robot Archie to get to the playground.
Write the codes using:

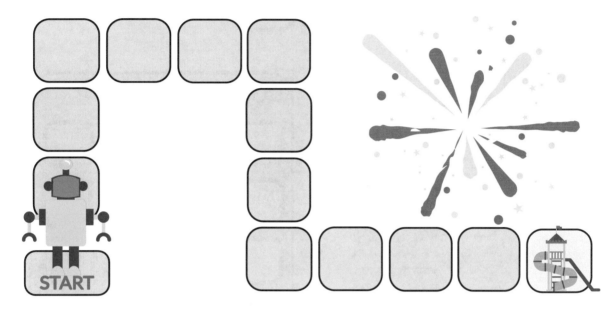

START

CODE:

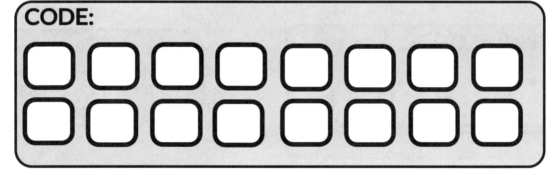

Let's try to write this code using LOOPS!

CODE with LOOPS:

Archie's way to the playground is getting more and more difficult.
He appreciates your help.
Write two codes for him. The first code without loops.
The second code with LOOPS. Use:

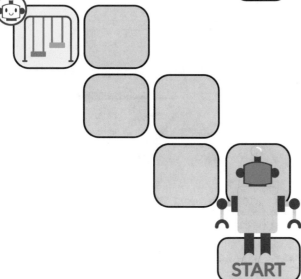

CODE:

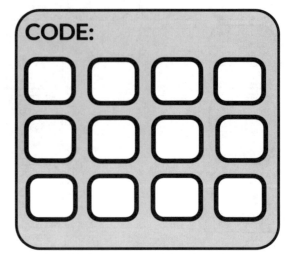

CODE with LOOPS:

TIP!
You need to include 4 moving blocks inside the LOOP.

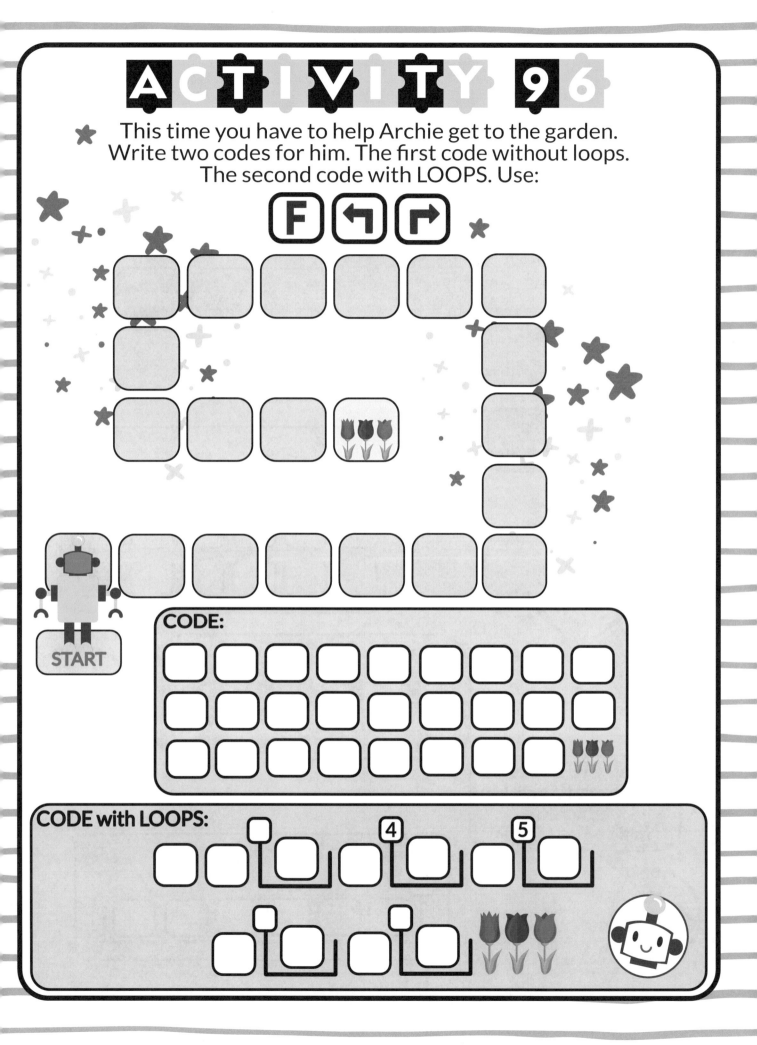

ACTIVITY 96

This time you have to help Archie get to the garden.
Write two codes for him. The first code without loops.
The second code with LOOPS. Use:

START

CODE:

CODE with LOOPS:

ACTIVITY 97

Archie's room is a mess. Help him to pick up all his toys. Write two codes for him. The first code without loops. The second code with LOOPS. Use:

START

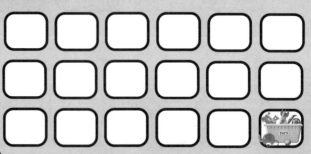

CODE:

SUPERB!

TIP!
You need to include 6 blocks inside the LOOP.

CODE with LOOPS:

Archie is going to visit his friend Max. There are three codes.
Which is correct?
Put a ✓ in a correct square (blue, yellow or pink).

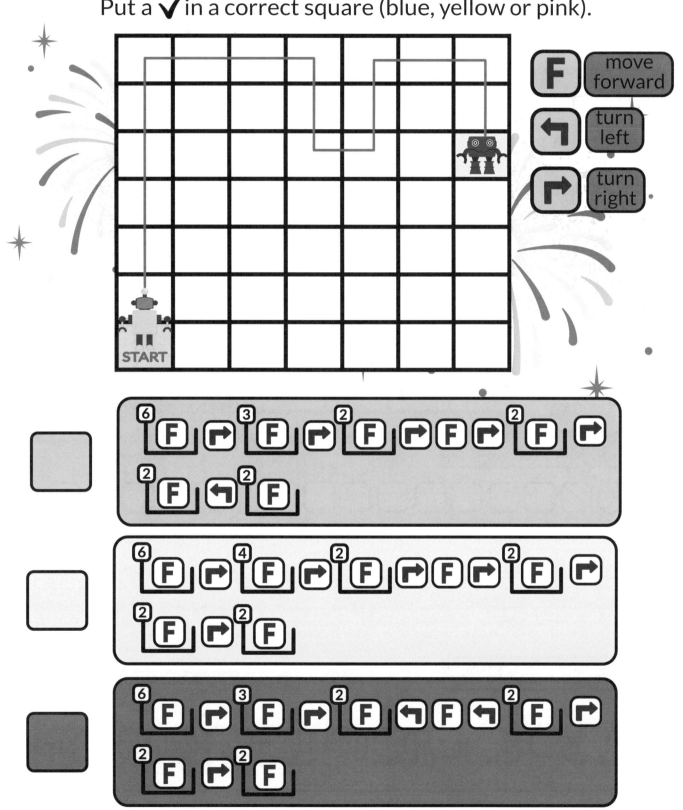

Archie is going to visit his friend Bob this time.
Write him the codes around the obstacles.

USE:

F move forward

turn left

turn right

 loop

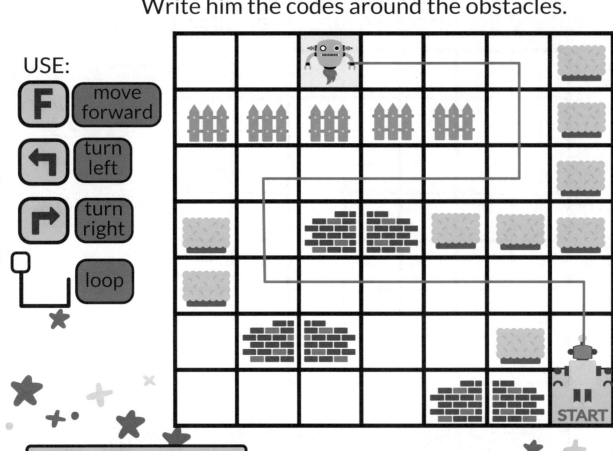

CODE without LOOPS

[ ] [ ] [ ] [ ] [ ] [ ] [ ] [ ] [ ] [ ] [ ] [ ] [ ] [ ] [ ] [ ]

[ ] [ ] [ ] [ ] [ ] [ ] [ ]

CODE with LOOPS

Archie has a secret message for you.
Try to decode it by following the code!

A	P	R	O	U	D	O	F	B	T	P	F	K	S	B
F	E	B	!	S	T	D	Y	S	L	E	U	Z	M	L
H	K	D	S	O	A	M	O	U	R	B	D	B	!	Z
G	J	W	N	G	R	Q	C	P	S	N	L	E	Q	K
Y	U	F	O	I	T	X	H	N	E	X	O	Y	O	U
M	I	Z	C	E	N	W	A	Z	L	Q	B	P	R	T
E	H	C	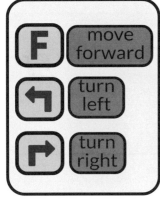	G	O	R	J	M	F	B	E	C	G	A

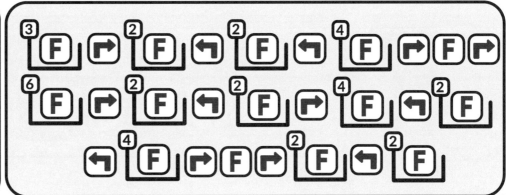

F	move forward
←	turn left
→	turn right

③ F → ② F ← ② F ← ④ F → F →
⑥ F → ② F ← ② F → ④ F ← ② F
④ ← F → F → ② F ← ② F

_____

_____

_____

_____

The Robots has one more message for you!
Decode it by following the code!

E	S	!	O	U	Z	O	F	L	T	P	F	U	B
M	E	S	U	F	O	R	Y	S	L	E	U	Z	N
H	G	D	O	O	A	B	D	U	R	B	D	G	!
A	N	K	Y	D	R	E	C	F	B	Q	K	J	Q
H	U	T	V	I	T	I	N	G	E	X	O	Y	H
T	I	Z	C	E	C	V	A	W	L	Q	B	L	R
	X	C	U	G	O	Q	J	I	T	H	U	S	!

F move forward

↰ turn left

↱ turn right

3 F ↱ 3 F ↰ 2 F ↱ 3 F ↱ 3 F

2 ↰ F ↱ 2 F ↰ 5 F

ANSWER KEY

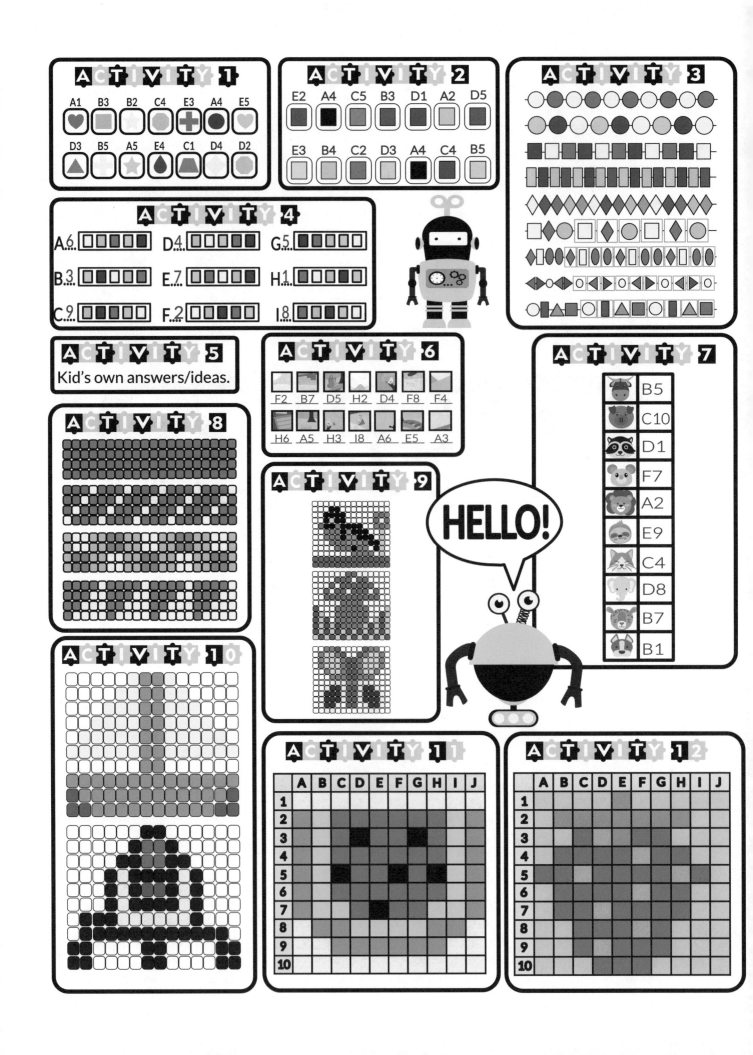

ACTIVITY 13

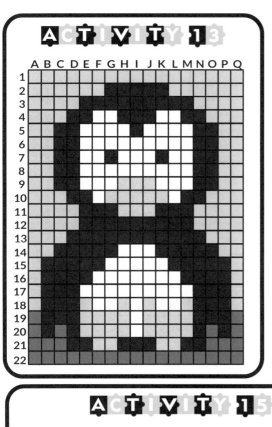

ACTIVITY 14

YOU'RE GREAT!

ACTIVITY 15

HOW MANY dinosaurs does Robot Olivier have?

18

HOW MANY dinosaurs does Robot Lucas have?

16

ACTIVITY 16

L	I	K	R	H
J	C	T	G	M
O	Z	S	N	E

ACTIVITY 18

B1	C1	C2	C3	B3	B4	C4	D4	D5	D6	D7	D8	E8	F8

ACTIVITY 17

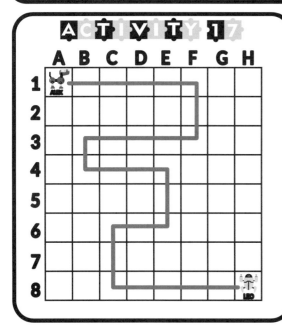

ACTIVITY 19

	←↑↑↑↑→→↑→→↑↑→→↑↑↑
	←↓↓↓→↑→→↓↓→→↑↑↑
✓	←←↑↑↑→↑→→↓↓→→↑↑↑

ACTIVITY 20

A8	B8	C8	D8	D7	D6	D5	E5	E4	E3	F3	G3	H3	H2
START	→	→	→	↑	↑	↑	↑	→	↑	↑	↑	→	↑

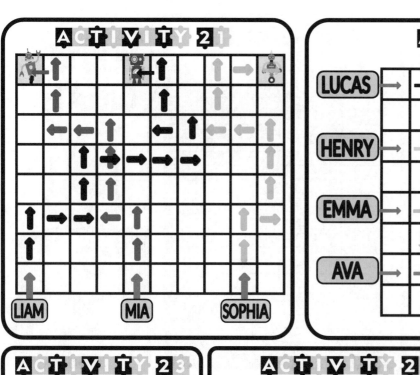

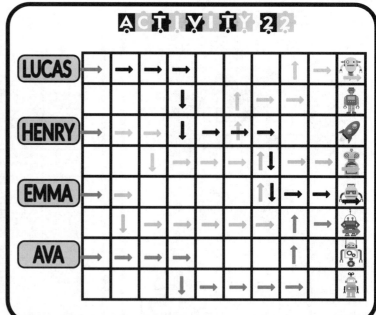

LIAM MIA SOPHIA

LUCAS HENRY EMMA AVA

1→ 1↓ 2→ 2↑ 1← 1↑

2→ 1↓ 1→ 2↓

3→ 2↓ 1← 1↓ 1←

3↓ 1→ 🍄 2↓ 🍄 2→ 1↑ 🍄 2→
1↑ 🍄 1↑ 3← 1↑ 🍄 1↑ 3→ 🍄

You are
gifted and
extraordinary

You can
do really
hard things

YOU ARE A......

C3	F7	A1	B6	E5	G2
C	L	E	V	E	R

B4	G7	E2	C1	D5	A6	G3
A	W	E	S	O	M	E

B1	A4	G6	G1	F4	D5	B7	E2	C3
C	O	N	F	I	D	E	N	T

D5	B4	F2
K	I	D

	1	3		7	5		7	1
	4	1		5	3		5	9
	10	8		2	9		10	2
	1	10		1	6		6	7
	8	8		7	10		9	10
	4	6		3	4		9	6
	10	4		2	2			

(x, y)	(x, y)
(2,4)	(3,1)
(1,3)	(4,2)
(2,1)	(2,3)
(4,2)	(4,4)
(4,4)	(1,5)
(3,3)	(1,1)
(1,2)	(3,5)

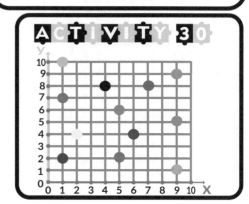

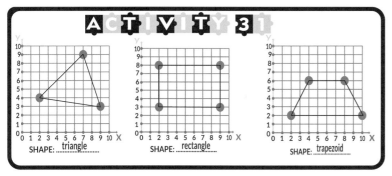

ACTIVITY 3 1

SHAPE: triangle

SHAPE: rectangle

SHAPE: trapezoid

ACTIVITY 3 2

	X	Y
	2	-2
	-2	-4
	-4	3
	-2	1

	X	Y
	4	-4
	2	2
	-3	5
	-2	-3

	X	Y
	-5	-3
	1	4
	1	-5
	4	5

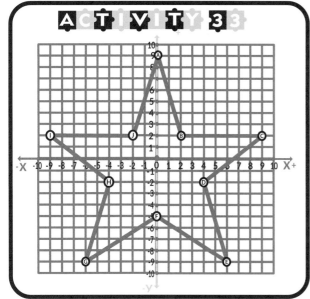

ACTIVITY 3 3

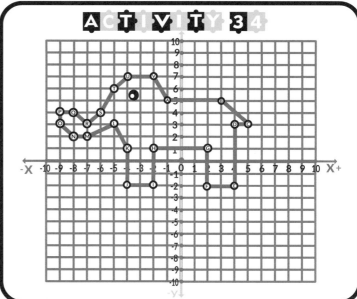

ACTIVITY 3 4

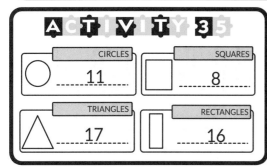

ACTIVITY 3 5

CIRCLES	11
SQUARES	8
TRIANGLES	17
RECTANGLES	16

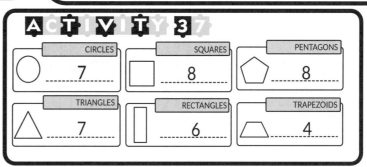

ACTIVITY 3 7

CIRCLES	7
SQUARES	8
PENTAGONS	8
TRIANGLES	7
RECTANGLES	6
TRAPEZOIDS	4

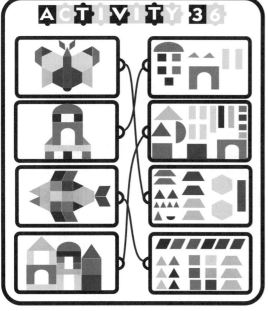

ACTIVITY 3 6

ACTIVITY 3 8

START

EXCELLENT!

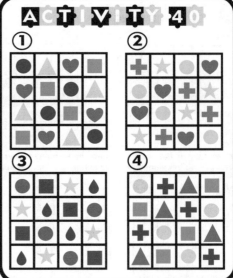

ACTIVITY 41

①

1	3	2	4
2	4	3	1
4	2	1	3
3	1	4	2

②

4	2	3	1
3	1	4	2
1	4	2	3
2	3	1	4

③

4	3	2	1
1	2	3	4
2	4	1	3
3	1	4	2

④

1	3	4	2
4	2	3	1
3	1	2	4
2	4	1	3

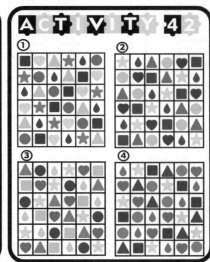

ACTIVITY 43

①

1	6	4	3	5	2
3	2	5	1	4	6
2	5	6	4	1	3
4	3	1	2	6	5
5	4	3	6	2	1
6	1	2	5	3	4

②

3	5	6	4	2	1
4	1	2	3	6	5
6	4	3	5	1	2
5	2	1	6	3	4
2	3	5	1	4	6
1	6	4	2	5	3

③

4	5	6	3	2	1
3	2	1	4	6	5
6	1	5	2	3	4
2	4	3	1	5	6
1	6	2	5	4	3
5	3	4	6	1	2

④

2	6	5	3	4	1
1	4	3	2	5	6
3	2	6	5	1	4
4	5	1	6	2	3
5	3	4	1	6	2
6	1	2	4	3	5

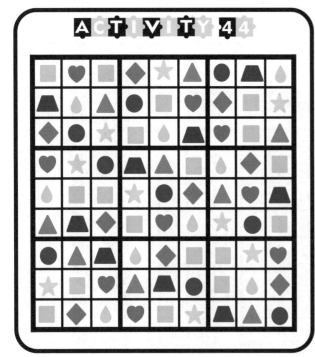

ACTIVITY 45

6	9	5	2	7	3	8	1	4
7	2	4	6	1	8	3	9	5
1	3	8	9	5	4	6	7	2
2	4	1	3	9	5	7	8	6
3	8	7	4	6	2	9	5	1
5	6	9	1	8	7	2	4	3
9	1	2	8	4	6	5	3	7
4	5	3	7	2	9	1	6	8
8	7	6	5	3	1	4	2	9

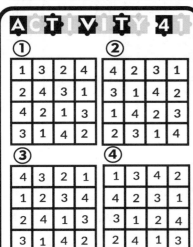

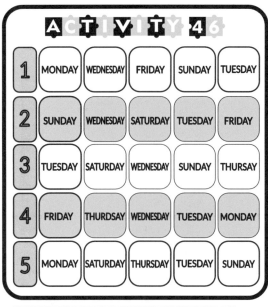

1	MONDAY	WEDNESDAY	FRIDAY	SUNDAY	TUESDAY
2	SUNDAY	WEDNESDAY	SATURDAY	TUESDAY	FRIDAY
3	TUESDAY	SATURDAY	WEDNESDAY	SUNDAY	THURSAY
4	FRIDAY	THURDSAY	WEDNESDAY	TUESDAY	MONDAY
5	MONDAY	SATURDAY	THURSDAY	TUESDAY	SUNDAY

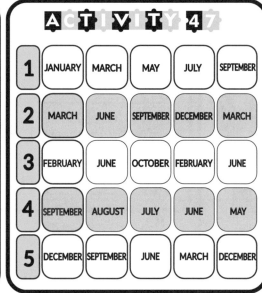

1	JANUARY	MARCH	MAY	JULY	SEPTEMBER
2	MARCH	JUNE	SEPTEMBER	DECEMBER	MARCH
3	FEBRUARY	JUNE	OCTOBER	FEBRUARY	JUNE
4	SEPTEMBER	AUGUST	JULY	JUNE	MAY
5	DECEMBER	SEPTEMBER	JUNE	MARCH	DECEMBER

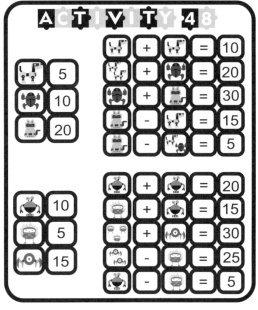

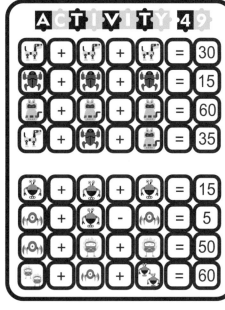

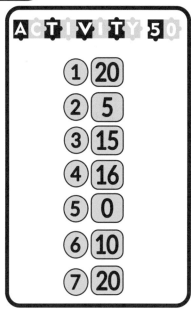

1) 20
2) 5
3) 15
4) 16
5) 0
6) 10
7) 20

1) 70
2) 55
3) 7
4) 30
5) 25
6) 57
7) 45

0010000100
0101001010
0101001010
1000110001
1000000001
1001001001
1000000001
0100110010
0100000010
0011111100

0110000110
1111001111
1111111111
1111111111
1111111111
1111111111
0111111110
0011111100
0001111000
0000110000

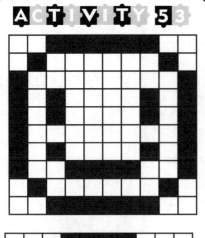

H	01001000		W	01010111		S	01010011
E	01000101		O	01001111		M	01001101
L	01001100		R	01010010		I	01001001
L	01001100		L	01001100		L	01001100
O	01001111		D	01000100		E	01000101

F	01000110
U	01010101
N	01001110
N	01001110
Y	01011001

B	01000010
R	01010010
A	01000001
V	01010110
E	01000101

J	01001010
O	01001111
Y	01011001
F	01000110
U	01010101
L	01001100

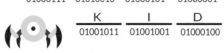

Y	O	U	A	R	E
01011001	01001111	01010101	01000001	01010010	01000101

S	U	C	H	A
01010011	01010101	01000011	01001000	01000001

G	R	E	A	T
01000111	01010010	01000101	01000001	01010100

K	I	D
01001011	01001001	01000100

D	R	E	A	M
01000100	01010010	01000101	01000001	01001101

B	I	G
01000010	01001001	01000111

N	E	V	E	R
01001110	01000101	01010110	01000101	01010010

G	I	V	E
01000111	01001001	01010110	01000101

U	P
01010101	01010000

Kid's own answers/ideas.

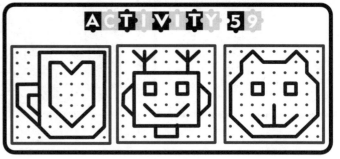

ACTIVITY 60

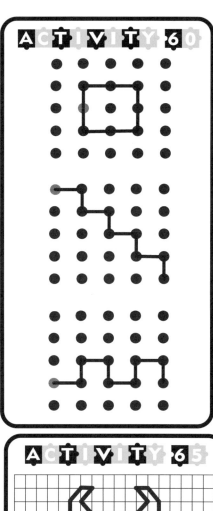

ACTIVITY 61

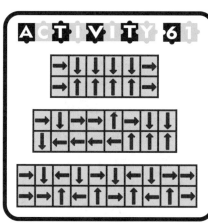

ACTIVITY 62

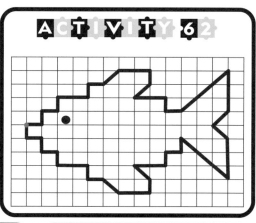

ACTIVITY 63

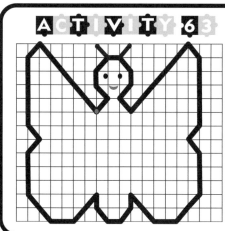

ACTIVITY 64

ACTIVITY 65

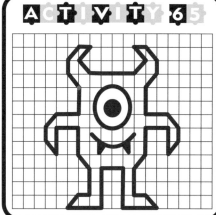

ACTIVITY 66

Butterfly
Ladybird
Grasshopper
Firefly

ACTIVITY 68

RAINBOW
UNICORN
DINOSAUR
MONSTER

ACTIVITY 67

You are one of a kind
Follow your dreams

ACTIVITY 69

YOU ARE SPECIAL
THE WORLD NEEDS YOU
YOU ARE STRONGER EVERYDAY

ACTIVITY 70

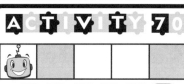

ACTIVITY 71

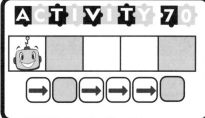

ACTIVITY 72

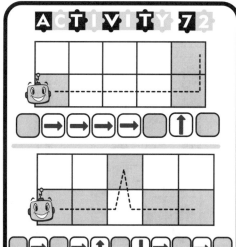

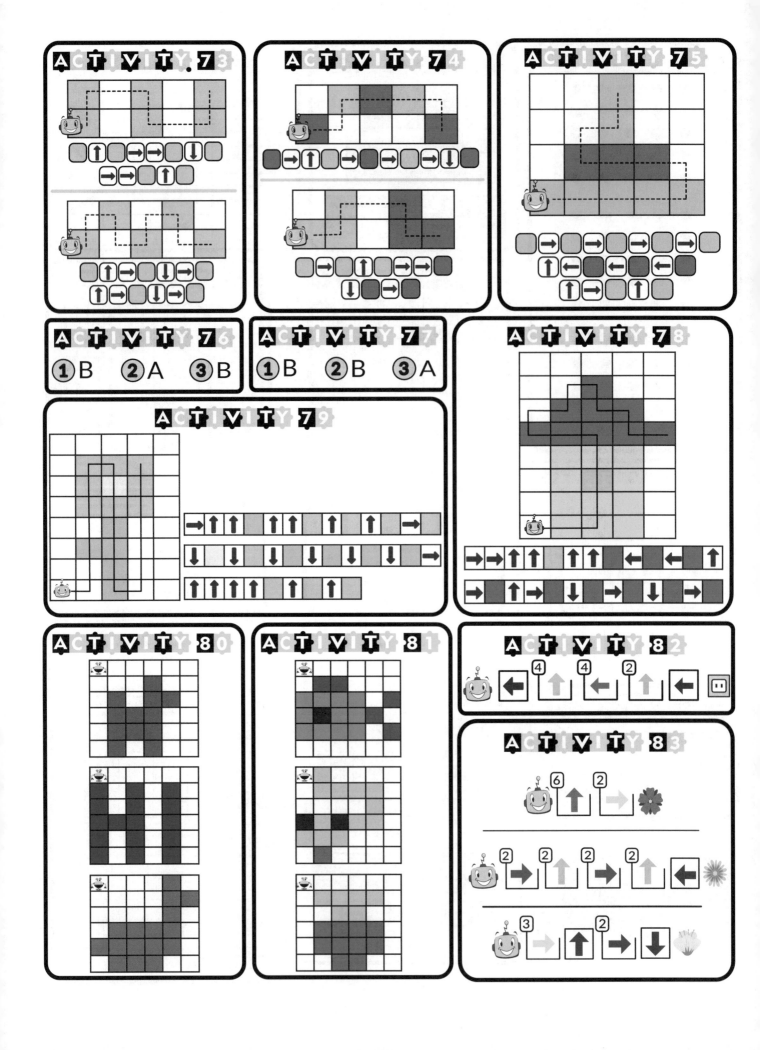

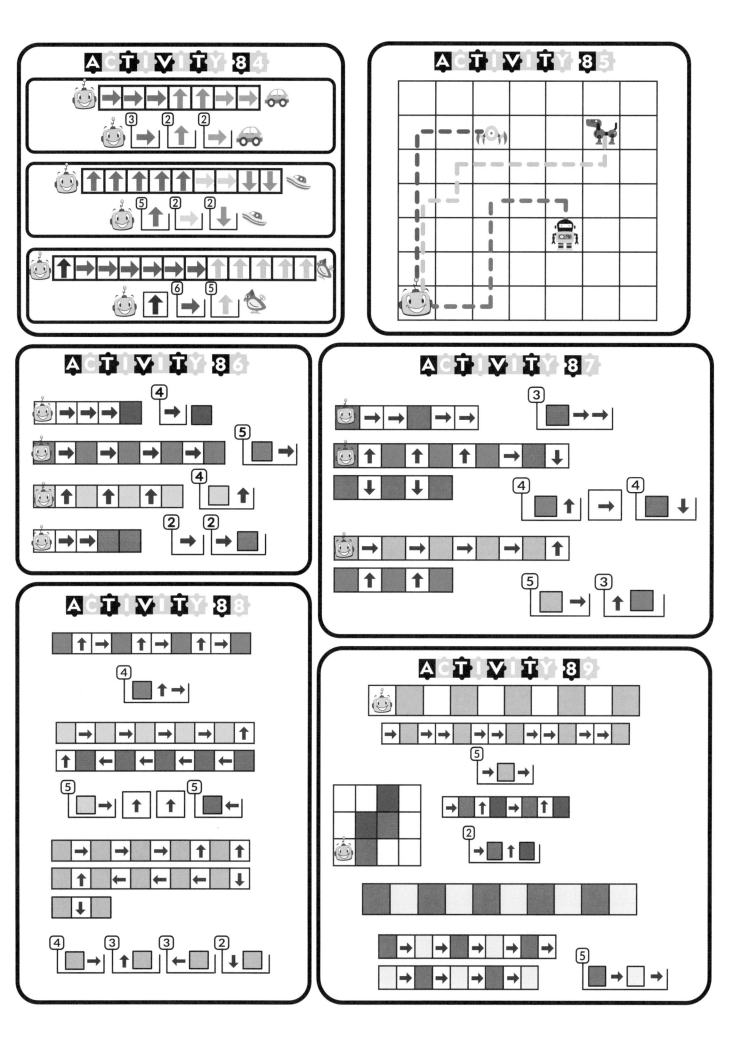

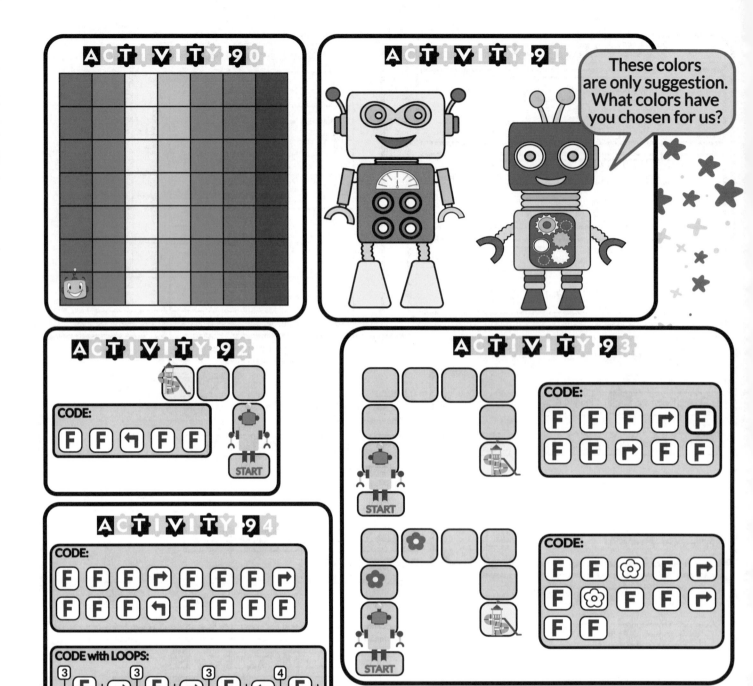

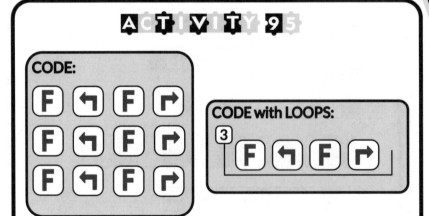

A	P	R	O	U	D	O	F	B	T	P	F	K	S	B
F	E	B	!	S	T	D	Y	S	L	E	U	Z	M	L
H	K	D	S	O	A	M	O	U	R	B	D	B	!	Z
G	J	W	N	G	R	Q	C	P	S	N	L	E	Q	K
Y	U	F	O	I	T	X	H	N	E	X	O	Y	O	U
M	I	Z	C	E	N	W	A	Z	L	Q	B	P	R	T
E	H	C		G	O	R	J	M	F	B	E	C	G	A

Congrats!
Be proud of yourself
Be bold
Be you

E	S	!	O	U	Z	O	F	L	T	P	F	U	B
M	E	S	U	F	O	R	Y	S	L	E	U	Z	N
H	G	D	O	O	A	B	D	U	R	B	D	G	!
A	N	K	Y	D	R	E	C	F	B	Q	K	J	Q
H	U	T	V	I	T	I	N	G	E	X	O	Y	H
T	I	Z	C	E	C	V	A	W	L	Q	B	L	R
	X	C	U	G	O	Q	J	I	T	H	U	S	!

Thank you
for being with us!

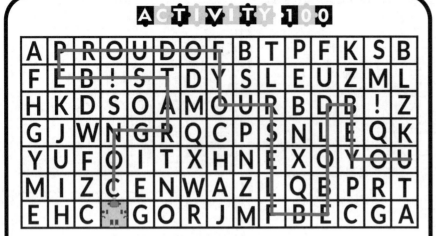

IT WAS GREAT TO MEET YOU!

FANTASTIC!

Made in United States
Troutdale, OR
10/30/2024